ESSAYS ON
DEVELOPING
ECONOMIES

ESSAYS ON DEVELOPING ECONOMIES

MICHAŁ KALECKI

With an Introduction by

JOAN ROBINSON

Emeritus Professor
of Economics,
Newnham College
University of Cambridge

THE HARVESTER PRESS

HUMANITIES PRESS

This edition first published in 1976 by
The Harvester Press Limited
Publisher: John Spiers
2 Stanford Terrace,
Hassocks, Sussex, England
and in the USA by
Humanities Press Inc.
Atlantic Highlands, New Jersey, N.J. 07716

Copyright © The Harvester Press Limited

Printed by Latimer Trend and Company Ltd.
Plymouth

The Harvester Press Ltd.
ISBN 0 85527 134 5

Library of Congress Cataloging in Publication Data

Kalecki, Michał.
    Essays on developing economies.

    Includes bibliographical references and Index.
    1. Underdeveloped areas—Economic policy—Addres-
ses, essays, lectures. 2. Economic development—Addresses,
essays, lectures. I Title.
HC59.7.K24 1976   338.91   75-40308
        ISBN 0-391-00524-3 (Humanities Press)

Contents

❋

5

Introduction

❋

Michał Kalecki's most notable contribution to economics was the discovery of the principle of effective demand in the setting of the great slump of the 1930s and of the possibility of curing unemployment, in an industrial economy, by government expenditure. The publication of Keynes's *General Theory of Employment Interest and Money* in 1936 stole the limelight, and the new interpretation of economic theory, which Kalecki had discovered independently, had been known ever since as the Keynesian revolution.

Kalecki never mentioned publicly that he had priority over Keynes. Long after the claim had been made for him by others, he prepared this characteristically terse reference to the fact in the introduction to a volume of selected essays.[1]

> The first part includes three papers published in 1933, 1934 and 1935 in Polish before Keynes's *General Theory* appeared, and containing, I believe, its essentials.

He died, however, before the volume was published.

Keynes had 'a long struggle to escape' from the neoclassical orthodox theory in which he had been brought up and there are some points at which the process was incomplete. Only the contortions of the neo-neoclassics, trying to reconstitute the old orthodoxy while accepting the main part of Keynes's theory, have shown how radical his departure from orthodoxy really was. It has become clear that Keynes's affinity in analysis, though not in ideology, is with the classical economists, and therefore with Marx, rather than with the tradition that he inherited from Marshall.

Kalecki had never learned the orthodox doctrine, and had no

need to escape from it. His insight into the cause of the break-down of the market economy could be immediately grafted on to Marx's schema of expanded reproduction, as he shows in the second paper in this volume. Kalecki is supplying the analysis of the realisation of the surplus which is somewhat confused in Marx.

With this background, Kalecki stresses, far more than Keynes, the political element in all economic developments and he brings into the centre of the argument the classical question, which Keynes was inclined to smooth over, of the division of the produce of the earth between the classes of the community.

Where Keynes has the concept of a psychological propensity to consume' which determines the amount of expenditure on consumption goods out of a given national income, Kalecki divides total income into wages and gross profits. Wages are consumed as they are received; total profits are derived from gross investment and rentier consumption. 'The workers spend what they get and the capitalists get what they spend.'

Keynes's analysis of the relation of the price level to the level of money–wage rates was based on a vague Marshallian conception of competition. Kalecki took imperfect competition into account. The ratio of gross margins to direct cost, in manufacturing industry, tends to be lower the more intense the competition between firms. The overall *share* of gross profit in value added depends on the 'degree of monopoly', while the *amount* of profit realised over a year depends upon capitalists' expenditure. All kinds of reservations and complications can be introduced into this model, but its simple form displays the essential relationship between the principle of effective demand and the distribution of income.

Perhaps it was for this reason that Kalecki's version of the theory was smothered in a conspiracy of silence in the USA, while Keynes's was accepted and, in a garbled form, incorporated into current teaching. Both were holding a mirror up to modern capitalism, but Keynes's mirror was somewhat misty while Kalecki's was too bright for comfort.

Kalecki had a wide experience of capitalist economies in depression, under wartime controls and in post-war prosperity, of the planned economy of Poland, and of a number of so-called 'developing' countries. In every case, he could diagnose the main problem in terms of his clear and penetrating scheme of ideas.

In the fifth paper in this volume, Kalecki outlines the principles of 'Keynesian' employment policy in a few pages. Under free enterprise, there is normally considerable slack in an industrial economy, with under-capacity operation of plant and under-employment of the labour force. This can be remedied by government expenditure. It is not necessary that this expenditure should lead to a budget deficit. In principle, it could be covered by taxation of the profits that it generates. Nor is it necessary that it should be devoted to so-called 'public works'. In principle, it could be used for the elimination of poverty. However, neither taxation of profits nor beneficial expenditure is agreeable to the interests and the ideology of the leaders of industry. The main vehicle for employment policy in the USA (and therefore for the capitalist world as a whole) has been expenditure on armaments.

At the present time, many economists and some industrialists, who for a long time welcomed the arms race as a useful means of fending off depression, are regretting that the slack was not taken up in a way that would have helped to relieve the menacing social poblems of modern capitalism. However, once the warfare state has become established it has powerful means of maintaining itself. Meanwhile, the plague has spread to the Third World; most so-called 'development' nowadays is devoted to so-called 'defence', which increases poverty rather than relieving it.

Non-employment in the underdeveloped economies is of a totally different nature from unemployment in the developed economies; it cannot be overcome merely by increasing effective demand. The objective of development is to increase productive capacity. To embark upon large schemes of investment without a coherent plan will mean a great deal of wasted effort. Moreover, even well directed investment sets up inflationary pressure. To avoid inflation requires a massive increase in the supply of necessities for consumption—in particular food—but at the same time investment itself enriches the old feudal and the new business families, deflecting resources into the produc-

tion of luxuries. A successful programme of development, therefore, requires strong measures to prevent growing inequality in
incomes.

The difficulties that beset the use of fiscal policy as a means of
controlling luxury consumption are briefly outlined in the third
paper and discussed in a formal manner in the seventh. Along
with the bold realism of his usual style of argument, Kalecki was
a master of the academic manner of precise analysis.

Kalecki's diagnosis seems unanswerable and later experience
has confirmed it, but it was not at all congenial to orthodox
opinion either in the wealthy countries, or among the intelligentsia in the Third World, who may admit the argument but
would lose by its implementation. Most of the 'development'
literature is aimed at disguising the truth of Kalecki's argument
and the greater part of 'development' policy consists, by open
war, of disguised pressure, in propping up regimes that can be
relied upon not to take the radical measures necessary for a
genuine development programme to get under way.

One of the most original and striking of Kalecki's conceptions
is the notion of 'intermediate regimes', in which the old feudal
class has been dispossessed and big business scarcely exists, so
that political power descends to the lower-middle class.

K. N. Raj has examined this conception in the Indian context.[2]
He points out that this new 'ruling class' is made up of many
disparate elements—rich peasants, small traders, educated
professional and civil servants—which have conflicting interests
amongst themselves. The government has to make itself responsible for investment but this type of regime is not favourable to
rapid development. Public enterprise is confined to basic
industries and is expected to sell its products and services at low
prices, leaving profitable markets to the small businesses. Taxation of agriculture is almost non-existent and taxation of the
urban sector is freely evaded. Thus funds for investment are hard
to extract. Both agriculture and manufactures fail to develop
efficiently, and whatever growth of national income is achieved
is mainly swallowed up in growing consumption.

The small industrial working class may be able to organise and
get some benefits for itself; the great mass of small peasants,
landless workers and the ever-growing numbers of unemployed,

scratching a bare living in the cities, dwell in a swamp of misery, but they do not pose a threat to the regime. Any attempt to organise these people politically is quickly crushed.

Some Marxists objected to Professor Raj's article, but Kalecki, and Raj after him, were attempting to use Marx's own method of analysis on problems that have come up since his day.

Mahmood Abdel Fadil finds that developments in Egypt can be interpreted in Kalecki's terms and he agrees with Kalecki that Egypt is closer than India to the archetypal case; local big business still plays some role in India, but almost none in Egypt. His study (to be published) promises to be an excellent example of the fruitful results to be obtained from following up Kalecki's original insights.

At the end of chapter 4 (p. 36–7) Kalecki recounts the brutal end of the experiment in Indonesia. Bolivia met a similar fate. Many small, nominally independent, nations in Africa and the Caribbean have succumbed to voluntary colonialism, inviting foreign capitalists to come and make profits out of local labour and resources. The situation in India grows more and more miserable, while Egypt is perhaps veering towards capitalism.

Kalecki foresaw that the intermediate regime is not likely to be a permanent system, but he was too optimistic in supposing that it might give birth to a viable socialist alternative.

Scattered throughout the papers are references to the contribution of overseas' finance to development. This is systematically discussed in the seventh paper, written in collaboration with Ignacy Sachs. Here, once more, Kalecki penetrates the mystifications that surround the subject in 'development' literature.

According to orthodox economic doctrine, 'capital' is a 'factor of production'. Loans or aid from wealthy countries provide 'capital' to the developing countries, which directly increases their productive capacity. Kalecki and Sachs point out that loans are not providing a 'factor of production' but means to finance a deficit in the balance of payments. This permits a surplus of imports for the time being, but in most cases the loans lead to obligations to pay interest which puts a burden on the balance of payments in the future. The contribution of finance to development depends upon the use to which the surplus imports are put and this in turn depends upon the effectiveness of control over the home economy and the success with which it is devoted to development. In so far as surplus imports are of luxury consumption goods, they cater for the tastes of a westernised élite and deflect home resources into imitating them. Imports of food have postponed the solution of the problem of home production, and this has created a desperate situation, now that imports are no longer available. Even imports of investment goods are not necessarily helpful to development. They are largely directed to expanding production of non-essential goods (deflecting home resources to be used in conjunction with them) and they generally embody techniques which are not the most appropriate for the receiving country.

Direct investment by foreign corporations is often included in 'aid'. This is clearly a misnomer. The investment is directed to what the corporations expect to be profitable, not to what the developing country most needs (cocacolonisation) and the right to remit profits in perpetuity makes this the most expensive of all forms of borrowing.

In the case studies, the general principles of Kalecki's analysis are applied to the advice which he was asked to offer to the authorities in particular countries. In one sense, they might now be thought to be out of date, for the particular situation that he was examining, in each case, has changed drastically since he wrote. All the same, they are still of great interest as exercises in the application of the principles of political economy to actual cases. Kalecki was far from being a 'pure theorist'. These reports are full of fascinating details, such as the use of home-made bricks in Israel to save imported cement, or the danger, in Cuba, of spoiling the taste of pork by using fish meal as feed for pigs.

The guarded thanks of the Minister of Finance of Israel show that Kalecki's home truths were sometimes painful and the policies that he recommended too strenuous to be popular. In any case, the problem that he was discussing has been overwhelmed by events before it was solved.

The tragic situation in India today shows the consequences of neglecting the policies that Kalecki was advocating in 1960. The 'intermediate regime' in Bolivia has succumbed to a military dictatorship which does not show any improvement in respect to economic policy.

Introduction

The case of the plan for Cuba is different from the others, since there a would-be socialist regime was already installed. Kalecki had to take over the estimate for agriculture from the Cuban authorities. He evidently had some reservations about it; it turned out to be excessively optimistic and so vitiated his own estimates of the possibilities of industrialisation. The Cuban government did not, in fact, adopt Kalecki's proposals for their first five year plan, which will come into operation in 1976. However, learning by trial and error rather than foreign advice, the Cuban economy is still pressing on and a socialist economy is growing from its own roots.

Cambridge   Joan Robinson
December, 1974

NOTES AND REFERENCES

1. *Selected Essays on the Dynamics of the Capitalist Economy*, Cambridge University Press, 1971.
2. *Economic and Political Weekly, Bombay*, 7 July, 1973.

I ECONOMIC PROBLEMS OF
UNDERDEVELOPED NON-SOCIALIST
ECONOMIES

I

Unemployment in Underdeveloped Countries*

❧

The problem of unemployment in underdeveloped countries differs fundamentally from that in developed capitalist economies. In the latter, unemployment arises on account of inadequacy of effective demand. During periods of depression unemployed labour coexists with underutilised equipment. The situation may, therefore, be tackled by measures designed to stimulate effective demand, such as loan financed government expenditure.

Unemployment and underemployment in underdeveloped countries are of an entirely different nature. They result from the shortage of capital equipment rather than from a deficiency of effective demand.

It may be asked, however, whether additional employment of a 'pick and shovel' variety, i.e. using only very little capital equipment, could not be created. Building and construction naturally provide an important avenue for this type of employment, but to some extent it may also be possible in the sphere of industrial production or services.

Here, however, we encounter the bottleneck of supply of necessities which depends on the inelasticity of agricultural production. Any increase in employment implies generation of additional incomes and thus, if no adequate increase in agricul-

* This is based on a seminar lecture delivered on 5th March 1960, under the auspices of the Indian Society of Labour Economics, at the Department of Economics, Lucknow University, Lucknow. Published in the *Indian Journal of Labour Economics*, III (2), July 1960, 59–61.

17

tural output is forthcoming, an inflationary increase in the prices of necessities will be unavoidable. The level of agricultural production sets, in the circumstances, a definite limit to employment possibilities even of a 'pick and shovel' variety.

Nothing is changed in this set-up by the fact that a large part of the additionally employed is drawn from the ranks of underemployed peasants, who are anyway consuming at a level equal to average productivity on the farm. Indeed, the demand for necessities increases, because either the wages of the newly employed will be higher than their previous consumption, or the income of the peasants who remain in agriculture will increase, or both.

The only possibility of avoiding inflationary pressure in the situation considered would be by levying taxes on low income groups or necessities, i.e. increasing employment at the expense of real wages. This method, however, militates against any sense of social justice: it is inadmissible to tax the poor rather than the rich on the ground that the latter would not consume fewer necessities under the impact of taxation.

Thus in order to tackle the problem of unemployment and underemployment in underdeveloped countries it is necessary to expand agricultural production rapidly. In conditions of rural overpopulation more intensive cultivation will make possible a *higher* transfer of labour from agriculture to other occupations. Indeed, up to a point, it will be possible to produce a higher output per acre with fewer people on the farm, without using labour saving techniques. At the same time the higher supply of food will make it possible to feed those who transfer to non-agricultural employment. Thus techniques which increase productivity per acre, eventually raise the productivity per man even more.

However, techniques which raise productivity per man without increasing productivity per acre do not contribute to the overall solution of the problem of employment. They may contribute to a higher surplus of agricultural products being available to urban areas, which would make it possible to augment employment there; but at the same time they would increase unemployment and underemployment in rural areas. Such would be, for instance, the consequences of establishing large-scale mechanised farms.

A substantial increase in agricultural output per acre may be achieved in underdeveloped countries without heavy investment and in a relatively short time, by such methods as small-scale irrigation, proper use of manure, double cropping, application of fertilisers and improved seeds, etc. The main obstacles to such an upsurge in agricultural production are the prevailing agrarian conditions.

In India, for instance, the development of agriculture is hampered to a considerable degree by:

(*a*) The inherent poverty of the small peasants enhanced by their dependence on the merchants and the money lenders.

(*b*) The operation of many farms under a system of disguised tenancy without security of tenure.

Thus the prerequisite of the rapid development of Indian agriculture is the overcoming of these institutional obstacles by government policies which aim at strengthening the smallholders, in particular relieving them of their dependence on the merchant and the money lender, and at granting security of tenure to the cultivators who still do not enjoy it. In the course of implementing such policies, service cooperatives could easily be created for the purpose of credit distribution, sale of produce, utilisation and establishment of irrigation facilities, etc.

It may be asked whether food imports could not facilitate considerably the solution of the problem of employment in underdeveloped countries. This, however, comes into consideration only for countries that are favourably endowed by nature with easily accessible mineral deposits, such as oil, which can provide a substantial volume of exports per head of population. Such conditions, however, are exceptional and in particular are unlikely to prevail in a large country. India in order to be in the position of Iraq, for example, would have to possess oil deposits sixty times greater than those of that country.

In general, the basic prerequisite for a rapid industrialisation of an underdeveloped country and in particular for the solution of the problem of unemployment and underemployment is a revolutionary upsurge in agricultural production.

2

The Difference between Crucial Economic Problems of Developed and Underdeveloped Non-Socialist Economies*

✻

I

The main problem of a developed capitalist economy is the adequacy of effective demand. Such an economy possesses a capital equipment which more or less matches the existing labour force, and therefore it could generate a rather high income *per capita* provided that its resources are fully used. This, however, is by no means necessarily the case. It was believed in the past that this occurs automatically, i.e. that such an economy tends to maintain full employment and thus unemployment may be considered merely an accidental short lived deviation from full utilisation of resources, an unimportant friction which may be disregarded. A basic revision in that view occurred during the great depression of the 1930s in which the capitalist system was shaken to its foundations. In fact, it is clear for us today that the problem of underutilisation of resources is, in a sense, inherent in a developed capitalist economy and that potentially, at least, it may emerge at any time.

* Address at the Reunion of Latin American Schools of Economics, Mexico City, June 1965. First published in M. Kalecki, *Essays on Planning and Economic Development*, PWN, Warsaw, 1968, 3, 9–18.

This is best shown by an examination of the position of full employment. A part of the full employment national product will be consumed by workers and a part by capitalists, but there will still be left a part that is not consumed, which corresponds to savings out of profits. (We abstract from savings of the workers, which are of no importance.) Now, if investment is so high as to absorb this surplus, full employment will be maintained. If, however, investment falls short of savings of capitalists then part of the product will remain unsold, and thus goods will accumulate on stock. In such a situation, it is obvious that the output of firms will be cut down until the level of the national income is reached at which saving is equal to the prevailing investment. The fall in the national income and employment will obviously cause a decline in consumption as well as in savings. It is now easy to see that the role of investment in establishing a certain level of national income is not associated with the final destination of the former: whether investment will prove useful or useless in the future, it generates the same effective demand when it is being carried out.

It is therefore perfectly obvious that investment may be replaced from the point of view of generating effective demand by government expenditures which are financed by loans, so that no reduction of any incomes by taxation is involved. Thus government expenditures based on budget deficit can solve the problem of effective demand; and if they are sufficiently high, they can assure full employment. This is the present basis of the government policy in modern capitalism. When investment falls short of the level which is necessary to maintain effective demand the gap is covered by government expenditure.

Now, it may appear queer that in this way one of the basic contradictions of the capitalist system is solved by a sort of financial trick. What, however, is queer is not this solution but the tendency for underemployment of resources through inadequate effective demand inherent in the capitalist system. This is best seen by a comparison with a socialist system, where the economic surplus is used by the government for capital formation; if, however, it does not choose to have such a high level of investment, it raises wages or reduces prices and thus correspondingly increases consumption. Such is not the position under the capitalist system. The artificiality of the under-employment of resources is overcome by the artificiality of the financial trick consisting of loan-financed *ad hoc* government expenditure.

Is it absolutely necessary to finance government expenditure by budget deficit in order to generate adequate effective demand? No. Indeed, imagine that full employment is achieved initially by budget deficit, but next the savings out of profits generated by this deficit are taxed away. In this way, profits are reduced to the levels that existed before the increase in government expenditure but nothing changes in the sphere of production. Thus government expenditure financed by a tax on profits may also ensure full employment. The difference as compared with deficit financing consists of the impact on profits after tax and its repercussions: in the case of budget deficit financing profits are increased by the amount of additional government expenditure which leads to an increase in capitalist consumption and in private investment. When government expenditure is financed by taxation of profits they remain unaltered and capitalists' consumption as well as private investment do not tend to rise.

Let us now consider the direction of government expenditure undertaken in order to maintain full employment. From the point of view of creating effective demand this does not matter as said above; the most rational course, however, and this would occur under a socialist system, would be to spend on investment and thus to accelerate the development of the economy; or to contribute through government expenditure (or reduction of taxation) to the increase in consumption of the broad masses of the population. However, under capitalism, this does not necessarily happen. Indeed, at present the available economic surplus is, to a great extent, used to produce armaments.

Thus the economy is kept going by armament expenditures and people are assured of their livelihood through the manufacture of the means of destruction. To an outsider, this looks fairly absurd, because the surplus could have been used to increase either investment or consumption. In fact however, it is wasted, or worse.

But, absurd though it is, even such a method of maintaining

22

full employment assures modern capitalism of a fair degree of political stability, because although the levels of mass consumption are not as high as they could be, they are still much higher than those that would prevail under conditions of unemployment. Moreover, if full employment is consistently maintained and if the relative share of labour in the national income remains constant, there will also be some continuous increase in the real wage because of the rising productivity of labour: if the labour force is continuously employed, if there is a rise in productivity and if the relative share of labour in the national income is unaltered, it is perfectly clear that the real wage is bound to rise. In this way the workers in developed countries achieve at present tolerable living conditions, which prevent them from revolting against the system which maintains full employment by a waste of resources endangering world peace.

II

The crucial problem of the underdeveloped economies is different from that of the developed countries. This is not to deny that in an underdeveloped economy there may be a deficiency of effective demand. There are many instances of countries whose capital equipment, meagre though it is, will nevertheless be underutilised. However, as contrasted with developed economies, even if this equipment is fully utilised, it is still not capable of absorbing all available labour, as a result of which the standard of living is very low. It is, of course, not very low for everybody, but such is certainly the case for the broad masses of the population. The situation cannot be remedied therefore by a financial trick; the main problem here being the deficiency of productive capacity rather than the anomaly of its underutilisation. Productive capacity should be not only fully utilised but rapidly expanded and this, as will be seen, is a much more difficult proposition.

The crucial problem facing the underdeveloped countries is thus to increase investment considerably, not for the sake of generating effective demand, as was the case in an underemployed developed economy, but for the sake of accelerating the expansion of productive capacity indispensable for the rapid growth of the national income. There will be, however, three important obstacles to stepping up investment. Firstly, it is possible that private investment will not be forthcoming at a desirable rate. Secondly, there may be no physical resources to produce more investment goods. Thirdly, even if the first two difficulties were overcome, there is still the problem of adequate supply of necessities to cover the demand resulting from the increase in employment.

Firstly, it is perfectly clear that, especially in underdeveloped countries, a high level of private investment is not easy to achieve. But we may assume that whenever private investment fails, the government steps in so that total investment reaches the desirable level.

Secondly, if the facilities to produce investment goods are fully used, it is impossible to increase their output in the period considered. But let us assume that such is not the case, that there exist some reserves in investment good industries, as contrasted with the consumer good sector (especially in construction).[1] Thus it would be still possible to increase investment.

Thirdly, if investment in this situation is increased, an inflationary pressure on necessities will arise because their supply, especially that of food, is limited. This cannot unfortunately be overcome through financing increased investment by taxation of profits. Such financing of investment ensures merely as shown above, that profits after tax will not rise and thus capitalist consumption will not tend to increase. However, because of higher employment there will be a pressure of wages on limited supplies of necessities and their prices will increase up to the point where the real value of the increased wage bill will be equal to the unchanged supply of necessities. Profits before tax will increase by the amount of the additional investment but this increment will be taxed away. In this way, both profits after tax and the real wage bill will remain unaltered. However, with increased employment more work will be done for the same real pay, i.e. the real wage per worker will decline, and it is this that will make possible a higher level of investment, which is a most unjust way of financing the increase necessary for the acceleration of economic growth.

The problems described above appear more tractable if they

are considered in terms of a long term plan rather than an abrupt acceleration of the expansion of productive capacity. In such a plan, we may envisage a gradual increase in investment in relation to the national income, as well as a gradual increase in the production of necessities.

Inflationary pressures may be avoided by planning an increase in the supply of necessities matching the demand for them, which will be generated by the planned increase in the national income. Apart from that, we shall face the problem of a gradually increasing relative share of investment in the national income as a counterpart of a gradual increase in the rate of growth of this income. This involves a reduction in the relative share of consumption in the national income, and in order to accomplish it in a fair way and to restrain the consumption of non-essentials, taxes should be imposed. Thus a gradual acceleration of the growth of the national income will be accompanied by an increase in the supply of necessities, adequate to prevent inflationary pressures; and the higher relative share of investment in the national income will be offset by a reduction of the relative share of non-essential consumption in this income achieved by appropriate direct or indirect taxation of the rich and the well-to-do.

III

This is a theoretical solution of the problem of balanced development of an underdeveloped mixed economy. It is easy to see, however, that the practical implementation of such a solution will encounter formidable political obstacles.

The first obstacle evolves simply from the problem of introducing some sort of planned economy. In such an economy, it will be necessary to plan not only the volume, but also the structure of investment; because, as said above, a proper allocation of investment between production of necessities, non-essentials and investment goods is indispensable. Now, this will obviously require a much deeper government intervention than that which aims at achieving full utilisation of existing resources in developed capitalist economies. On the one hand, the government will have to invest in all branches of the economy in which adequate private investment will not be forthcoming. On the other, private investment will have to be licensed in order to prevent the upward deviation of actual investment in some sectors of the economy from the planned level.

The next and most difficult task is that of ensuring a proper increase in the supply of necessities. Imagine that in the plan appropriate investment is allocated both to agriculture and to the manufacture of fertilisers, which are necessary to achieve the planned increase in the production of food. This does not, however, solve the problem fully. The point is that in an underdeveloped economy agricultural production is beset with a variety of limitations, which would prevent it from growing at a high rate even if all material resources were available. These powerful obstacles to the development of agriculture are the feudal or semi-feudal relations in land tenure as well as the domination of the poor peasants by merchants and money lenders. Thus a radical acceleration of the development of agriculture is impossible if substantial institutional changes are not introduced. Nor would an agrarian reform be sufficient for the purpose because, as is shown by experience, even after the agrarian reform has been carried out, there remains the dependence of the peasants on money lenders and merchants, not to mention the circumvention of the reform itself. It is perfectly clear that overcoming the resistance to such institutional changes by the privileged classes is a much more difficult proposition than the financial trick which solves the problem of effective demand crucial for the developed economies.

Finally, there arises the problem of adequate taxation of the rich and well-to-do to make room for higher investment. Here again serious obstacles are encountered. Tax collection in underdeveloped economies is very difficult and tax evasion is rampant, even when the respective laws are passed. This is also used as an argument against introduction of the taxes in question by the vested interests concerned. As a result not much progress is usually made in this matter.

The three problems discussed above—the intervention of the government in the sphere of investment with the aim of securing its planned volume and structure, the overcoming of the institutional barriers to rapid development of agriculture, and adequate taxation of the rich and well-to-do—clearly present a formidable political problem. In theory, most people will approve of the economic necessity of undertaking the measures in question, even including many representatives of the ruling classes. But when it comes to their implementation, affecting all sorts of vested interests, the situation changes radically and a formidable counteraction develops in a variety of ways. For, as a matter of fact, the overcoming of all the obstacles to economic development enumerated above amounts to more than the upheaval created in the eighteenth century by the French Revolution. Thus it is not surprising that these reforms are not peacefully carried out.

Vigorous but balanced development of the type outlined above is hardly encountered in practice. In fact we find two types of development (perhaps with some intermediate cases) : either the development is non-inflationary, but extremely slow, or it is relatively rapid and is accompanied by violent inflationary pressures. This is the actual reason for the political tension in underdeveloped countries which is kept in check by military dictatorships or more subtle devices. It may be seen now that the difference between highly developed and underdeveloped nonsocialist economies can be formulated in a very simple way. In one case, existing resources have to be utilised and modern capitalism has learned the trick of doing it. In the other case, resources have to be built up and this requires far-reaching reforms amounting to revolutionary changes. This simple fact explains the difference in the economic and political situations in these two groups of countries and, in a sense, determines the present phase of history.

NOTES AND REFERENCES

1.   In fact, a sizeable proportion of investment goods is obtained through foreign trade and it may be imagined that an increase in investment is partly secured through some expansion of exports or a reduction of imports of non-essentials.

3

*The Difference between Perspective Planning in Socialist and Mixed Economies**

✻

My paper on the construction of a perspective plan which has been accepted for this session is based on Polish experience and therefore it applies fully only to a socialist economy.† It is useful to consider briefly here some important additional problems which arise when similar planning methods are applied to the so-called 'mixed economies'.

As stated in my paper, even in a socialist economy the rate of growth of particular sectors is limited for technical and organisational reasons, so that an increase in capital outlay will not be helpful in raising the rate of expansion of output beyond a certain level. In a mixed economy, there will be, in addition, powerful institutional factors impeding the growth of some sectors of the economy. In particular, such will be the case in agriculture, where agrarian conditions, such as feudal land ownership and domination of peasants by merchants and money lenders, keep down the rate of growth of agricultural production. The resulting low rate of expansion of the supply of food either

* Intervention made as head of the Polish delegation at the United Nations conference on the Application of Science and Technology for the Benefit of Less Developed Regions, Geneva 1963. First published in M. Kalecki, *Essays on Planning and Economic Development*, PWN, Warsaw, 1963, I, 21–2.

† Cf. ibid., 9–21.

limits the growth of the national income or causes inflationary increases in the prices of necessities.

Another problem facing mixed economies, as contrasted with socialist economies, is that of directing the investment in the private sector. In some cases, investment may prove inadequate in particular branches of industry which are essential for a successful implementation of the plan; in other cases private investment which is taking place may prove excessive or undesirable as, for instance, that in luxury residential construction.

Finally, the problem of financing economic development in a mixed economy differs in some aspects from that in a socialist economy. In the latter, the relevant problem is the contradiction between the fast rate of growth assuring high consumption standards in the longer run and the level of consumption in the near future. But once the government has taken a compromise decision on the subject, the problem of financing investment is resolved simply by appropriate fixing of prices and wages. The position in a mixed economy is different in so far as government investment is financed to a considerable extent by taxation. Now, direct or indirect taxation of the poor, as long as the very rich are in existence, is inequitable. But the very rich, the well-to-do and, last but not least, the foreign companies, resist the imposition of taxes which affect them by their political influence upon the government; and even if the respective laws are passed, they nevertheless manage frequently to evade them. The result is, in part, the shifting of the burden of financing investment to the poor and, in part, the restriction of the possibilities of accumulation.

The difficulties facing the mixed economies in their economic development which were enumerated here may not be insuperable. However, it is necessary to allow in perspective planning for basic policies aiming at overcoming these institutional obstacles to rapid economic growth.

4

Observations on Social and Economic Aspects of 'Intermediate Regimes'*

❀

I

History has shown that lower-middle class and rich peasantry are rather unlikely to perform the role of the ruling class. Whenever social upheavals did enable representatives of these classes to rise to power, they invariably served the interests of big business (often allied with the remnants of the feudal system). This despite the fact that there is a basic contradiction between the interests of the lower-middle class and big business, to mention only the displacement of small firms by business concerns.

Are there any specific conditions today favouring the emergence of governments representing the interests of the lower-middle class (including in this also the corresponding strata of the peasantry)? It would seem that such conditions do arise at present in many underdeveloped countries.

(*a*) At the time of achieving independence the lower-middle class is very numerous while big business is predominantly foreign controlled with a rather small participation of native capitalists.

(*b*) Patterns of government economic activities are now widespread. Apart from the obvious case of socialist countries, state

* First published in *Coexistence*, IV (1), 1967, 1–5.

economic interventionism plays an important role in developed capitalist countries.

(*c*) It is possible to obtain foreign capital also through credits granted by socialist countries.

II

In the process of political emancipation—especially if this is not accompanied by armed struggle—representatives of the lower-middle class rise in a way naturally to power.

To keep in power they must:

(*a*) Achieve not only political but also economic emancipation, i.e. gain a measure of independence from foreign capital.

(*b*) Carry out a land reform.

(*c*) Assure continuous economic growth.

This last point is closely connected with the other two.

By endeavouring at least to limit foreign influence, the lower-middle class government heads into conflict with the 'comprador' elements. When carrying out a land reform it clashes with the feudal landlords. However, it may not necessarily be inclined to defy the native upper-middle class. Reliance of this class in the strategy of economic development could easily result in the repetition of a well-known historical pattern—the final submission of the lower-middle class to the interests of big business. This, however, is prevented by the weakness of the native upper-middle class and its inability to perform the role of 'dynamic entrepreneurs' on a large-scale. The basic investment for economic development must therefore be carried out by the state, which leads directly to the pattern of amalgamation of the interests of the lower-middle class with state capitalism.

The realisation of this pattern is facilitated by the participation of the state in the management of the economy, a phenomenon characteristic of our era. A large part of the world population today lives in the centrally planned socialist economies. But also in the developed capitalist countries, there prevails today a fair measure of state interventionism, which at the very least is aimed at preventing the business downswings.

We are all 'planners' today, although very different in character. No wonder, then, that the underdeveloped countries, striving to expand their economic potential as fast as possible (while the main concern of the developed capitalist countries is to utilise fully the available productive capacity) tend to draw up plans of economic development. The next step is to provide for a large volume of investment in the public sector, since, as shown by experience, private initiative cannot be relied upon to undertake an adequate volume of investment of appropriate structure. Thus state capitalism is closely connected with planning of one form or another which underdeveloped countries can hardly avoid today.

Evolution in this direction could be counteracted significantly by the pressure of the imperialist countries, exerted by attaching appropriate 'strings' to credits granted. Since underdeveloped countries cannot do without some inflow of foreign capital, pressure of this kind could be highly effective in changing the lower-middle class governments into servile tools of big business allied with the feudal class. Apart from an 'ideological' victory, imperialist countries would gain a better foothold for defending their 'old' investments in underdeveloped countries and for a 'new' expansion in this sphere. A significant obstacle to these imperialist pressures, though, is the possibility of obtaining credits from socialist countries. Its effect is reflected not merely in the amount of capital actually received by underdeveloped countries from this source, but also in strengthening their bargaining position in dealing with the financial capitalist powers. The competition with the socialist countries for influence in the intermediate regimes forces those powers to grant credits without attaching conditions as to the internal economic policy, although the imperialist governments do try to obtain as much as possible in this respect.

III

The social system in which the lower-middle class cooperates with state capitalism calls for a somewhat more detailed discussion. To be sure, this system is highly advantageous to the lower-middle class and the rich peasants; state capitalism concentrates investment on the expansion of the productive potential of the country. Thus there is no danger of forcing the small firms out of business, which is a characteristic feature of the early stage of industrialisation under *laissez faire*. Next, the rapid development of state enterprises creates executive and technical openings for ambitious young men of the numerous ruling class. Finally, the land reform, which is not preceded by an agrarian revolution, is conducted in such a way that the middle class which directly exploits the poor peasants—i.e. the money lenders and merchants—maintains its position, while the rich peasantry achieves considerable gains in the process.

The antagonists of the ruling class are, from above, the upper-middle class allied with foreign capital and the feudal land-owners and, from below, the small landholders and landless peasants, as well as the poor urban population—workers in small factories and the unemployed or casually employed, mainly migrants from the countryside in search of a source of livelihood. On the other hand, white-collar workers and the not very numerous workers of large establishments—who in under-developed countries are in a privileged position as compared with the urban and rural paupers—are frequently, especially when employed in state enterprises, allies of the lower-middle class rather than its antagonists.

IV

As to the antagonistic 'higher' classes, the feudals are generally deprived of political significance by the land reform. They may retain parts of their land through fictitious sales to relatives (so as to evade the ceiling) but this does not put them in a strong position in the political and social life of the country. On the other hand, the relation to the upper-middle class may range from far-reaching nationalisation (usually with compensation) to a mere limitation of the scope of private investment coupled with attempts, as a rule rather ineffective, to adjust its structure to the general goals of development.

The political importance of big business in the country corresponds to these variants. In any case its tendency to oppose the government is checked by the fear of the urban and rural proletariat, from which it is effectively separated by the ruling lower-middle class. The choice of the particular variant of dealing with big business is determined not so much by the ideology of the ruling class, as by the strength of the former. Without taking into consideration the existing economic conditions, one might expect more 'socialism' from a Nehru than from a Nasser. It was, however, the other way round, because at the time of gaining political independence, big business in India was much stronger than in Egypt.

V

Potentially at least, the urban and rural paupers are antagonistic towards the ruling class, since they do not benefit from the change of social system such as described above, and profit relatively little from economic development. The land reform is conducted in such a way that a major share of the land available goes to the rich and medium-rich peasants while the small landholders and the rural proletariat receive only very little land. Insufficient effort is made to free the poor peasantry from the clutches of money lenders and merchants and to raise the wages of farm labourers. The resulting agrarian situation is one of the factors limiting agricultural output within the general economic development, as under the prevailing agrarian relations the small farms are unable to expand their production. The same is true of larger farms cultivated by tenants. The lagging of agriculture behind general economic growth leads to an inadequate supply of foodstuffs and an increase in their prices, which is again to the disadvantage of the 'stepsons' of the system. Even if the aggregate real incomes of those strata do not decline as a result of the increase in employment, they do not show any appreciable growth.

Though the poorest strata of the society have thus no reason to be happy, they do not, for the time being at least, constitute a danger for the present system. The poor peasantry and rural proletariat are controlled by some form of a local oligarchy comprised of the petty bourgeoisie (merchants and money lenders), the richer peasants and smaller landlords. The urban population without stable employment, and even home workers and workers in small factories are not too dangerous either, because they are permanently threatened by unemployment and are difficult to organise.

In this context, one can easily understand the repressions against the communists observable in a number of intermediate regimes. This is not a question of competition between parallel ideologies; the communists are simply at least potential spokesmen for the rural and urban paupers, and the lower-middle class is quite rightly afraid of the political activisation of the latter.

It is true that this lower-middle class and the prosperous peasants are not really rich; in many instances their standard of living is lower than that of workers in developed countries. But in comparison to the masses of poor peasants, who also flood the cities as unemployed or badly-paid home workers, the petty bourgeois is a tycoon with a lot to lose. In this context, it is no coincidence either that the governments in question favour religion—even to the point of adopting an official religion—and show a tendency towards external expansion and militarism associated with it.

VI

On the international scene, the internal position of the ruling lower-middle class finds its counterpart in the policy of neutrality between the two blocs; an alliance with any of the blocs would strengthen the corresponding antagonist at home. At the same time, the neutrality is very important in the context of foreign credits mentioned above.

The intermediate regimes are the proverbial clever calves that suck two cows; each bloc gives them financial aid competing with the other. Thus has been made possible the 'miracle' of getting out of the USA some credits with no strings attached as to internal economic policy.

It should still be noticed that foreign credits are of great importance to the intermediate regimes. The lagging of their agriculture behind their overall development—caused to a great extent by institutional factors—results in a shortage of foodstuffs which the state covers partly by imports (since the paupers must not be pushed to extremes). This creates additional difficulties in the already strained balance of payments for which the remedy is sought in foreign credits.

Such a position in international relations defends the intermediate regimes, as said above, against the pressure from imperialist powers aimed at restoration of the 'normal' rule of big business, in which foreign capital would play an appreciable role (though more limited than in the past). Without such external pressures it is highly unlikely that the amalgamation of lower-middle class with state capitalism could be destroyed and classical capitalism reinstated.

* * *

The above was published in Poland at the end of 1964. Although Indonesia did not at that time contradict the pattern of intermediate regimes we outlined, it was by no means its representative example and this for the following reasons.

(*a*) In economic policy, Indonesia lagged considerably behind a typical intermediate regime. The agrarian reform was in actual fact fairly ineffective and changed relatively little in Indonesian agrarian conditions. Nor did the government make any consistent effort in terms of industrialisation and planning; in particular, a violent inflation was permitted to develop. More than that, the government made a point of granting priority to 'national integration' (inclusive of the claims to West Irian and Northern Borneo) over economic and social problems.

(*b*) On the other side, the foreign policy of Indonesia was more anti-imperialist and anti-colonialist than that of other intermediate regimes. This radicalism was partly associated with the territorial claims mentioned above (in particular with 'confrontation with Malaysia') but was definitely general in character.

(*c*) The by-product of the fight for incorporation of West Irian and of the 'confrontation with Malaysia' was the expansion of the army—which, *inter alia*, imposed a considerable burden on the economy—and the enhancing of the political power of its higher echelons.

(*d*) As contrasted with other intermediate regimes, Indonesia had a very large communist party. It was rooted mainly in the dissatisfaction of the poor peasants and farm labourers. However, it cooperated with the regime on the basis of support for its anti-imperialist policies, without militating strongly against its neglect of domestic economic and social problems and not being prepared for a showdown with the reactionary middle classes closely associated with the army. It is obvious that the communist party represented here a much greater threat to these classes than in other intermediate regimes, which, however, was still potential rather than actual.

It is the situation outlined above that created the basis for subsequent developments in Indonesia. The full history of the events of 30 September 1965 has not yet been written. So much is clear—that the communists did not attempt a takeover and that, in fact, these events played the role of a *Reichstagsfeuer*. The anti-communist terror that followed was unprecedented even in the history of counterrevolutions: in the space of a few months about 400,000 people were murdered. The higher echelons of the army largely representing the reactionary middle class and rich peasants, or even semi-feudal elements, thus eliminated the 'anomaly' of a powerful communist party in an intermediate regime.

The foreign policy also swung back to 'normal'. Although, as said above, the army derived a great measure of their power from the policy of confrontation with Malaysia, it is they who have now terminated this policy. In general the radicalism of Indonesian foreign policy is over, although, at least for the time being, the non-alignment policy has not been abolished.

The economic problems which are emphasised by the new government are being blamed on their predecessors. However, the conclusions drawn from the catastrophic economic situation do not point at all to more planning or agrarian reform. The terror that rages against not only communists but radicals in general is probably considered an adequate substitute for progressive economic and social policies.

II FINANCING ECONOMIC DEVELOPMENT

5

The Problem of
Financing Economic
Development*

❃

I

At the first stage of our analysis we shall deal with a simplified
model. We shall assume that the economic system is closed and
that government expenditure and revenue are negligible. This
obviously does not correspond to the real situation in underdeveloped countries. Such countries usually depend to a great
extent on foreign trade, and public expenditure and revenue
are no less important than in developed countries. It will be
seen, however, that from the consideration of such a simplified
model conclusions may be derived elucidating the mechanism
of the financing of investment in the course of economic development. It will be seen, moreover, that it is rather easy to amend
these conclusions when simplified assumptions are dropped by
stages.

We shall distinguish in our model the following social classes:
capitalists, workers and small proprietors. The last group includes poorer peasants, artisans, small shopkeepers, etc. It will
be assumed that both small proprietors and workers do not save,
and that their consumption is equal to their income. While the

* This article is a summary, revised by the author, of lectures which he
gave in the *Centro de Estudios Monetarios Latinoamericanos*, Mexico City, in
August 1953. Kalecki was at that time an official of the Department of
Economic Affairs of the United Nations. The article was published in Spanish
in the *El Trimestre Economico, Mexico*, October–December, 1954, and in
English in the *Indian Economic Review*, February 1955, II (3), 1–22.

assumption of no saving is realistic for this group, it may happen frequently that some 'dissaving' takes place. This may be especially true of poorer peasants. For the sake of simplicity we shall, however, abstract from this factor and thus we shall assume that workers and small proprietors consume all their income and no more.[1] Under this assumption the total saving is equal to the saving out of profits of the capitalists.

We shall subdivide the economy into two sectors producing investment and consumption goods, respectively. In each sector, we shall include the production of the respective commodities from the lowest stage. Thus, production of raw materials and fuel will be allocated between the two sectors according to the uses that are made of them in the production of final products. We shall denote the investment goods sector as Department I and the consumption goods sector as Department II.

Investment stands here not only for the production of investment goods for the sake of replacement and expansion of plant and equipment, but also for the accumulation of inventories. We shall include the production corresponding to the accumulation of inventories, even of consumption goods, in Department I. This somewhat artificial classification is introduced to make investment and consumption coincide with the output of Department I and Department II, respectively, which simplifies considerably the subsequent argument.

We shall now derive the basic exchange interrelation between the two departments. Let us consider these departments in a given unit period (e.g., in a given year). In both departments, part of the value of the product will be consumed and part will be saved. We shall also include in saving depreciation funds, so that our saving means gross saving, just as our investment means gross investment. In this way, the value of the production of each sector will be split between consumption, which we denote by C_1 or C_2, and saving, which we denote by S_1 or S_2. Thus, the value of production of Department I will be equal to $C_1 + S_1$, i.e. the sum of consumption and saving derived out of incomes received in Department I. Similarly, the value of production of Department II will be equal to $C_2 + S_2$. Consumption in Department I (C_1) is, of course, supplied out of the production of Department II. This happens as follows. Part of the production of consumption goods in Department I is consumed in that department by workers, small proprietors and also by capitalists. But as the latter do not consume all their profits, a surplus of consumption goods is produed in that department corresponding to the unconsumed part of profits, i.e. corresponding to the saving in this department (S_2). It is obvious, therefore, that consumption in Department I is equal to the saving in Department II

$$C_1 = S_2. \tag{1}$$

In other words, the surplus of consumption goods in Department II is sold to the workers and capitalists in Department I. (The accumulation of unsold goods in Department II cannot interfere with this equation because by definition the accumulation of inventories is included in Department I.)

This basic equation can be found in the discussion of expandded reproduction schemes by Marx. It may be shown also that this equation is equivalent to the equality between savings and investment. Indeed, if we add savings in Department I (S_1) to both sides of the equation we have

$$C_1 + S_1 = S_2 + S_1 \tag{2}$$

Now, the left-hand side is nothing else but the value of production of Department I or investment (I). The right-hand side of the equation is the sum of the savings in both departments, or the total savings (S). Thus, equation 2 is equivalent to

$$I = S. \tag{3}$$

This equation shows that, in a sense, investment finances itself. Indeed, imagine that investment in the course of its execution is financed by banking credit or out of liquid reserves of firms; it will be seen that investment as it is carried out creates its counterpart in saving. A part of saving arises directly in Department I. The second part of saving is the equivalent of the selling of the surplus of consumption goods of Department II to workers and capitalists in Department I. These savings, which accrue to entrepreneurs who profited from the demand generated by higher investment, accumulate as deposits. If investment is financed out of liquid reserves of the entrepreneurs concerned, the process will result in a shift of deposits from these entrepreneurs to other capitalists. If investment is financed by short term bank credit, the savings accruing in the form of deposits will be available for absorption of the issue of debentures and shares by the investing entrepreneurs. Thus the latter are able to repay the bank credits involved. Finally, if investment is financed by long term bank credit, the saving, being the counterpart of the higher investment, will swell the deposits or will be used for repayment of bank credits.

There are no financial limits, in the formal sense, to the volume of investment. The real problem is whether this financing of investment does, or does not, create inflationary pressures. For the consideration of this problem the most convenient is our first equation (1).

It is easy to show that the crucial point in the problem of whether a certain level of investment creates or does not create inflationary pressures is the possibility of expansion of supply of consumer goods in response to demand. To elucidate this problem let us consider two extreme cases.

Let us assume, firstly, that while investment is increased, output of consumption goods cannot be stepped up because the productive capacities are fully utilised at the beginning of the period considered and no expansion in these capacities has taken place in this period. In such a case the increase in demand for consumption goods in Department I would cause an increase in prices of these goods. The prices will rise up to the point where the saved profits (S_2) will be equal to C_1 and real wages will fall. (Small proprietors in Department II will not necessarily profit from the rise in prices either, because the profits may accrue to the capitalists on whom they depend, i.e. merchants, money lenders, etc.). This is the case which is sometimes called in economic writings 'forced savings'. The reaction of workers to the reduction of real wages will be a demand for higher money wages, and thus a price–wage spiral will be initiated.

Let us now consider another extreme case. Let us assume that sufficient capacity is available to meet the increased demand for consumption goods from Department I. This may be the case either because at the beginning of the period in which the increase in investment takes place there was adequate productive capacity in Department II,[2] or because, in the course of this period, adequate additions were made to this capacity as a result of the process of economic development. In such a case, it will not be the prices but production that will be pushed up, to the point where S_2 is equal to C_1. In other words, the output of Department II will increase to such an extent that the surplus in this department corresponding to the part of profits that is not consumed (S_2) will be equal to the increased C_1 at constant prices.

In the next section we shall consider in more detail the problem of inflationary pressures generated by investment. Prior to this, however, we shall generalise somewhat the above argument by dropping one of the simplifying assumptions. We have assumed so far that government expenditure and revenue are negligible. We shall allow now for public investment. Since we shall assume, however, for the time being that it is fully financed by government loans, we shall continue to abstract from government revenue as well as from government administrative expenditure.

We shall allow for loan financed public investment by modifying the meaning of I. In what follows, I will stand not only for private investment but also for public investment, and the respective production will be assumed to be included in Department I. It is easy to see that despite this modification of the meaning of I, the preceding equations, and in particular the equality between investment and saving, will hold good if public investment is fully financed by loans. The process of such financing will indeed not differ from that of private investment. The increase in production of Department I on account of public investment will push production or prices in Department II up to the point where the increase in consumption in Department I (C_1) will be equal to the increase in saving in Department II (S_2). Public investment, if financed by loans, will thus generate, just as private investment does, its counterpart in saving. Let us assume that the government finances investment initially by loans from the banking system. The disbursement of the respective sums will generate an equal amount of liquid saving, which will then be available for taking up government securities and thus will make possible the funding of the loan. If, however, such securities are not issued, this saving will swell the deposits or will be used for repayment of private bank credits. Here again the problem of inflationary pressure will depend merely on the conditions of supply of consumption goods.

These results are of considerable importance. We concentrated above on the subject of repercussions on the economy of an increase in private investment, especially on the problem of the conditions under which this increase does, or does not, give rise to inflationary pressures. It should be noted, however, that the problem of the 'danger of inflation' may not arise at all, because the entrepreneurs may for various reasons tend to keep their investment at a low level. Investment may be limited not because of the difficulties of financing its increase without causing inflation, but by the unwillingness of the entrepreneurs to expand their capital expenditures. In such a situation, public investment acquires a crucial importance for the process of rapid economic development and the fact that its repercussions, even when financed by loans, do not generate higher inflationary pressures than private investment is highly significant.[3]

II

We considered above the two extreme cases of the elasticity of supply of consumption goods, which are rather simple. Actually the situation is more complicated because in some sectors of Department II the supply of consumption goods may be elastic and in some it is rigid. An important instance of this situation in underdeveloped countries is the case where the supply of industrial consumption goods is elastic because considerable reserves of productive capacity exist or because it may not require a very large investment to increase that capacity. On the other hand, the supply of food may be fairly rigid. This will depend on the fact that under the conditions prevailing in underdeveloped countries food production expands in response to demand less than in developed countries.[4]

One factor seems to make for a relief in the demand pressure on limited food supplies as a result of an increase in industrial employment, but this effect proves to be, at least in part, only apparent. In underdeveloped countries, the additional labour force will frequently come from rural districts. In many instances, agricultural production will not fall, as a result of the existence of 'surplus labour' in agriculture. It may thus be surmised that no difficulties in supply will arise because the migration from the countryside will leave behind an extra surplus of food which will find its way to the urban markets. This, however, is not correct because a large proportion of this extra surplus will frequently be used to increase the food consumption of the peasants. In addition, the standard of living of an industrial worker will frequently be higher than that of a poor peasant. Thus the demand generated by higher employment will only in part be met by the extra surplus created in the course of migration.

It follows from the above that the rise in investment may create a strong pressure on the available supplies of food, while at the same time it is possible to increase the production of industrial consumption goods in line with demand. It may be shown that in some instances the rigidity of the supply of food may lead to the underutilisation of productive facilities in non-food consumption goods. This will not be the case if the peasants profit from the increases in food prices, because then they buy more industrial consumption goods out of their higher incomes. However, if the benefits of higher food prices accrue to landlords, merchants or money lenders, then the reduction in real wages due to the increase in food prices will not have as a counterpart an increased demand for mass consumption goods on the part of the countryside; for increased profits will not be spent at all, or will be spent on luxuries. In this case, the high demand generated by a rapid development involving large scale investment will not create a market for industrial mass consumption goods. As is clearly seen from the above, two factors will be involved here:

(*a*) The inelastic supply of food leading to a fall in real wages.

(*b*) The benefit of food price increases accruing not to small proprietors, but to capitalists.

It is of some interest to put this case into a more general perspective. It should be noted that it was the lack of adequate markets that was frequently considered the main obstacle of development rather than the dangers of inflation. The problem was usually formulated as follows. In view of the small internal demand, there will be no outlet for the products of the newly built factories. Thus industrialisation will prove impossible unless it is oriented towards external markets. The answer to this problem is provided by the argument in section I. If investment is sufficiently high, it pushes the demand for consumption goods up to the point where the surplus of these goods in Department II meets the higher demand of workers and capitalists in Department I. In this way, it is the high level of investment itself that generates demand for consumption goods. It still remains true that the *initial* impetus for investment frequently comes from external demand or from government intervention and that, even in the later stages, private investment may be supplemented by public capital expenditure. Assuming, however, a high and rising level of investment, the problem of the market is solved and there even arises the problem of inflation if the pace of industrialisation is rapid. But closer analysis indicates in turn that the 'danger of inflation' is by no means incompatible with the market problem; the latter is apt to reappear if the supply of food is rigid and the conditions of the distribution of income in agriculture are such as described above.

We can conclude that the increase in investment under conditions of inelastic food supply will cause a fall in real wages and will generate an inflationary price–wage spiral. Moreover, this type of inflation may not be associated with any considerable rise in demand for industrial consumption goods. Thus, it is clear from the above that the expansion of food production, paralleling the industrial development, is of paramount importance for avoiding inflationary pressures. Investment in industry, transportation, public utilities and even long run development projects in agriculture should be accompanied by measures which will expand agricultural production in the short period. These measures range from land reform and cheap bank credit for peasants to improvements in the method of cultivation, small-scale irrigation and cheap fertilisers.[5]

While an adequate supply of food is of basic importance for preventing inflation, in the course of economic development, the increases in industrial productivity work in the same direction. There is, however, an important difference. An increase in the supply of food tends to raise real wages at a given level of non-agricultural employment. On the other hand, an increase in productivity tends to increase real wages through a reduction of the level of employment corresponding to a given level of non-agricultural production. Let us now consider the latter process in more detail.

Imagine that there is a significant increase in productivity throughout the non-agricultural sector in both Department I and Department II. As a result, employment corresponding to a given level of production in that sector will fall in inverse proportion. This will cause a proportionate fall of the wage bill at given wage rates. The demand for food will thus be reduced proportionately and food prices will decline. If the distribution of income between capitalists and workers in industry remains unchanged, prices of industrial products will also decline roughly in proportion to productivity. The final result will thus be a fall both in industrial and agricultural prices with given wage rates and thus a rise in real wages. It is of course clear from the above that at the same time the process of transfer of labour from the agricultural to the industrial sector will be slowed down.

In order to put the effect of changes in productivity into a proper perspective, it may be useful to consider two extreme examples. Let us first assume that agricultural production remains stationary and that all increases in industrial production are achieved by using more capital per worker, which results in a rise in productivity. In such an economy, the problem of inflation will not arise. The prices of industrial goods will tend to fall because of the rise in productivity. The consequent rise in real wages will increase the demand for food, and that will cause some rise in food prices. But this rise cannot be so high as to eliminate the increase in real wages, since then the very cause of the higher demand for food would disappear. Thus real wages will rise to some extent, and so will peasants' incomes, because of higher prices of agricultural products[6] and lower prices of industrial commodities. But the situation is not so favourable as it would appear from this description, because there would be no shift of population from the countryside to the town, which is one of the main causes of the increase in the standard of living in the course of economic development. Disguised unemployment would not be reduced, and the country would be split into two sectors: primitive agriculture and modern industry. The other extreme is the case where productivity does not increase at all and the increase in industrial production is achieved merely through a shift of population from the rural to the urban districts. In such a case, disguised unemployment would be diminishing radically, but at the same time considerable inflationary pressures are likely to develop, because it may be difficult to expand agricultural production so as to satisfy the rapidly rising urban demand. The optimum pattern usually falls between these two extremes; the increase in industrial production should be based on the rise both in productivity and in employment.

In the above argument, we made an assumption that the distribution of income between workers and capitalists in industry will remain unchanged while productivity increases. This need not, of course, be the case if there is a rise in the degree of monopoly which causes a shift to profits. Such a phenomenon may, of course, occur quite independently of the increase in productivity. Since, in the course of economic development, there will be a tendency towards increased concentration in industry, a rise in the degree of monopoly may easily take place. Moreover, if development involves considerable direct investment by foreign capitalists, the practices of industrial monopolies or quasi-monopolies are brought from developed to under-developed countries. What will be the repercussions of an increase in the degree of monopoly? The rise of prices in relation to wages will reduce effective demand and prevent the full utilisation of industrial facilities. It is true that this decline in real wages will diminish the pressure on agricultural supplies, but the ensuing fall in food prices cannot be so great as to restore the real wages, or its very cause would disappear. The final result will be a shift in the distribution of income from wages and agricultural incomes to industrial profits. The case shows some similarity to that considered above, where real wages fell because of the increases in food prices while the benefits of these increases accrued to merchants, landlords or money lenders. In both cases, the process tends to keep down the demand for industrial mass consumption goods as a result of a shift to profits in the distribution of income. However, in the present case it is the monopolistic industrialists who will reap the benefit.

In the above analysis, the inelasticity of supply in agriculture and the monopolistic tendencies in industry emerge as important factors underlying inflationary effects in the course of rapid economic development. The rise in productivity mitigates inflationary pressures, but at the same time it slows down the rate at which surplus rural labour is absorbed into industry.

III

The above considerations were based on the following simplifying assumptions: we abstracted from foreign trade and from government administrative expenditure and revenue while public investment was assumed to be financed by loans. We shall now introduce foreign trade into our model, but we shall assume for the time being that it is balanced, i.e. that exports are equal to imports. We shall also allow for government administrative expenditure, but we shall again assume that it is balanced by government revenue so that public investment will continue to be loan financed.

Let us allow first for balanced foreign trade. For this purpose we shall modify our model as follows. We split all export industries proportionately to the imports of investment goods and consumption goods which are obtained in exchange for exports. We next allocate these two parts to Department I and Department II, respectively. Thus, Department I will now include, in addition to the industries producing investment goods, export industries which produce exports of a value equal to the imports of investment goods. Similarly, Department II will include the production of consumption goods plus the production of export goods which provides for imports of consumption goods. It is clear that also in this model there will hold good the equality between consumption in Department I and saving in Department II $(C_1 = S_2)$, and thus the equality of investment and saving $(I = S)$.

It will be easily seen that the relation between employment in Department I and the volume of investment will depend now not only on the productivity of labour, but also on the terms of trade. The better the terms of trade the higher, *ceteris paribus*, will be the volume of investment in relation to employment in Department I. Similarly, the supply of consumption goods in relation to employment in Department II will be higher the better are the terms of trade. Thus to the same level of employment there corresponds a higher investment and a lower pressure of demand. It follows directly that an improvement in the terms of trade will reduce the inflationary pressures corresponding to a given level of investment.

It should be noted that an even more important aspect of the better terms of trade is their contribution to the equilibrium between imports and exports. Indeed, rapid economic development is apt to create a strain on the foreign balance. Imports will tend to increase for various reasons:

(*a*) The rise in investment will require considerably higher imports of capital goods which cannot be produced at home.

(*b*) The increase in total industrial production will involve higher imports of foreign raw materials and semi-manufactures.

(*c*) The difficulty of increasing food production *pari passu* with demand may also necessitate importation of food.

An offsetting factor is the increased self-sufficiency with regard to industrial mass consumption goods, but this will hardly compensate for the higher demand due to the above factors, especially in the first stage of the accelerated development. At the same time it may be difficult to increase exports in step with imports. Firstly, such an expansion may require considerable capital resources and thus with a given level of investment may slow down the development oriented toward the internal market. Secondly, it may not be easy to enter foreign markets on a larger scale without causing a deterioration in the terms of trade. Because of the strain in the balance of payments resulting from all these factors, import restrictions designed to minimise importation of non-essentials are almost inevitably a concomitant of vigorous economic development.

We shall next introduce into our model government expenditure and revenue. Let us first introduce the administrative budget, which we assume to be balanced, i.e. we assume that administrative expenditure is equal to revenue. We shall, moreover, assume for the sake of simplicity that all the administrative expenditure is on the salaries of officials and that these officials do not save, so that their consumption is equal to their salaries. Let us denote the total tax revenue by T, the taxes, both direct and indirect, paid by Department I (i.e. by capitalists, small proprietors and workers of this department) by T_1 and all taxes paid by Department II by T_2. Total consumption of the officials, according to the above assumptions, will be equal to the total amount of tax revenue (T). Therefore, the demand for consumption goods originating outside Department II is equal to the consumption in Department I (C_1) plus the total tax revenue (T). On the other hand, the surplus of consumption goods over consumption in Department II is now equal to $T_2 + S_2$, because this surplus now corresponds not only to the savings of capitalists of Department II but also to taxes paid by this department. As a result, equation 1 is now modified into an equation

$$C_1 + T = T_2 + S_2. \tag{4}$$

If we deduct T_2 from both sides of equation 4, we shall obtain

$$C_1 + T_1 = S_2 \tag{5}$$

because T is equal to $T_1 + T_2$. If, moreover, we add to both sides of equation 5 the saving in Department I, we shall obtain

$$C_1 + T_1 + S_1 = S_2 + S_1. \tag{6}$$

The left-hand side of equation 6 is nothing else but the total value of production of Department I, or investment (I). The right-hand side of the equation is equal to the total saving (S). We therefore obtain again the equality between investment and saving $(I = S)$. Thus, in this case, the process of investment again automatically creates a counterpart in saving. Production of consumption goods or their prices will be pushed up to a point where the surplus of consumption goods in Department II, equivalent to taxes paid there and the savings of capitalists of that department, will equal the demand for consumption goods coming from Department I and government officials.

It is clear that the higher government expenditure and revenue, the lower, *ceteris paribus*, will be the real wages after taxation. This is clear in the case where the taxes are paid directly by workers or in the case of indirect taxation. But it will be true even in the case of direct taxes paid by capitalists. These taxes will partly come out of capitalists' savings, and to this extent the demand for consumption goods will not be reduced, and an additional pressure on the available supply of consumption goods will be generated.

Thus lower government administrative expenditure and revenue will mitigate the inflationary repercussions of rapid economic development and consequently the reduction of the administrative budget will tend to benefit the process of development. It should be noted, however, that the cuts in expenditure should not impair the functioning of economic agencies which are necessary for furthering this process.

The model which we have built up gradually is characterised by balanced foreign trade, a balanced administrative budget, and by public investment financed fully by loans. This model is very much closer to reality than that adopted as a first approximation. However, even the present model may still require modifications. Foreign trade may not be balanced, since imports may exceed exports because of the import of capital. Moreover, tax revenue may exceed administrative expenditure, so that a part or all of public expenditure is financed by taxation. In both cases, the modifications would tend to relieve inflationary pressures which may be caused by rapid economic development. We shall therefore consider the problems involved in some detail.

IV

We shall discuss below the effect of capital imports, which, as said above, tend to relieve the inflationary pressures corresponding to a given level of investment.

Let us denote the import of capital which is equal to the deficit in foreign trade by F. If the import of capital is used for purchasing investment goods abroad, it is clear that the same amount of investment will be achieved by a smaller production of investment goods at home and thus the pressure on the supply of consumption goods will be *pro tanto* relieved. If we denote the total investment by I, we shall have the equation

$$I = S + F \tag{7}$$

which shows that a smaller amount of saving is now necessary to finance a given amount of investment.

If the import of capital is used for purchasing consumption goods abroad, it appears that the same equation holds good. Indeed, for the case of balanced trade we had equation 4. Since an additional supply of consumption goods equal to the foreign trade deficit (F) will now be available, we shall have

$$C_1 + T = T_2 + S_2 + F. \qquad (8)$$

From this follows, taking into consideration that total taxes (T) are equal to $T_1 + T_2$,

$$C_1 + T_1 = S_2 + F. \qquad (9)$$

Adding S_1 to both sides of the equation, we obtain

$$C_1 + T_1 + S_1 = S_2 + S_1 + F. \qquad (10)$$

Or, finally,

$$I = S + F. \qquad (7)$$

In the case in which capital imports are used to purchase investment goods abroad, the amount of investment goods to be produced at home in order to achieve a given level of total investment is *pro tanto* reduced, and the pressure of demand on supply is relieved from the demand side. If the capital imports are used to purchase consumption goods abroad, the pressure of demand on supply is reduced from the supply side. In both cases, however, the amount of home saving necessary to finance investment is reduced by the total amount of imported capital and thus inflationary pressures are correspondingly relieved.

Another function of capital imports is to relieve the shortage of foreign exchange. Indeed, as mentioned above, the process of development tends to strain the balance of payments by raising the requirements for imports of capital goods as a result of higher investment, the requirements for imports of industrial raw materials because of growing industrial production, and the requirements for imports of food if home production lags behind demand.

The above shows the advantages of importing capital for the rapid development of a country. In practice, however, this way of financing economic development presents problems which are frequently insuperable. From a purely economic point of view, the interest paid on the imported capital will burden the balance of payments in the future, which means both a loss of resources and also a risk of balance of payments difficulties. This problem is, of course, the more acute the higher the rate of interest. But even more important is the question of the availability of foreign capital which will not involve problems of a more basic nature.

The import of capital may take three forms: grants, loans or direct investment. It is clear that, from the purely economic point of view, grants would be the most preferred form, because they would not raise the *economic* difficulties mentioned above. However, some political strings would usually be attached to such grants as would be available on a large scale, and this may adversely affect the whole course of development.

Let us consider in turn the problem of direct investment. It is sometimes maintained that such investment is preferable to loans because the rate of dividend on shares is flexible according to the business situation, while the rate of interest on bonds is not. It should be noticed, however, that this is offset by the fact that the former rate is usually, on the average, much higher than the latter. More important still are the general economic and political aspects of direct investment. Direct investment frequently takes place in certain branches of the economy, such as the production of raw materials for export, which may not be in line with a reasonable plan for the development of the resources of a country. It will give to that development a one-sided twist. But apart from that, the big concerns engaged in this investment will inevitably acquire considerable political influence upon the governments concerned, and the consequences of this may easily vitiate the process of economic development.

Thus, the most suitable type of imports of capital for the development of a country are foreign loans obtained on a purely commercial basis; but such loans may have the economic disadvantage of a rather high rate of interest and will be hard to obtain, because of the danger of future difficulties in the balance of payments which may render the transferability of the interest and amortization impossible. These difficulties may perhaps be remedied in some instances in the following way. Transactions may be imagined where investment goods from abroad are obtained on loan, the repayment of and the interest on which take the form of future exports of specific commodities produced in the underdeveloped country in question. In this way the future balance of payments difficulties connected with amortization and interest payments on loans are eliminated to some extent, because the foreign exchange for the respective payments need not be obtained in the world market. Such arrangements may be of advantage to the lending country, which on the one hand has an unutilised capacity in the manufacture of investment goods, and on the other hand is keen on securing the future flow of raw materials.

The above makes clear the difficulty of securing imports of capital from developed to underdeveloped countries on acceptable terms. Perhaps a partial substitute may be found in preventing the *export* of capital from underdeveloped to developed countries, which is by no means negligible. Not only must the flight of visible capital be taken into consideration here, but also the hidden transfers, which are frequently of even greater importance. A common method, for instance, of circumventing exchange restrictions is to understate export prices and to overstate import prices. (The same practice is frequently used, especially by foreign companies, in order to make export profits appear lower.) The elimination of such abuses may indeed yield sizeable amounts of 'foreign capital'.

Another similar way of securing foreign capital is to cut down the transfers of dividends abroad by existing foreign enterprises. This, in fact, has been done in many countries, by taxation of export profits in this or other forms; by blocking the transfers of dividends abroad, either partly or fully and, in some cases, by nationalisation of the enterprises concerned. The argument frequently used against such policies is that they discourage direct foreign investment. If, however, a rather sceptical attitude is taken, as above, with regard to the role of direct foreign investment in economic development, this argument loses much of its weight.[7]

The difficulties of securing foreign capital in a form favourable to development explain the importance which is attributed in underdeveloped countries to improving the terms of trade. We have already briefly considered their significance for economic development. It is interesting to look at them now from the point of view of a comparison with capital imports. Any improvement in terms of trade may be considered equivalent to the import of capital, without the difficulties accompanying the latter. This is obvious with regard to the supply of foreign exchange, because all the additional exchange obtained through an improvement

57

in the terms of trade may be mobilised by the government for additional purchases essential for development. As to the internal repercussions, they may be rendered identical with those of a foreign loan, by imposing export duties when the improvement in terms of trade is due to the rise in export prices, or import duties when it is due to the fall in import prices. If the duties in question are exactly equal to the change in foreign prices, they clearly leave the internal situation unaffected, while investment increases by the amount of the gain in foreign exchange.

The last stage of the argument leads up to the problem of the influence of taxation on the repercussions of investment undertaken in the course of economic development. We shall now deal with this problem.

V

We shall now turn to the subject of taxation as an anti-inflationary measure. It has been assumed so far that the administrative budget is balanced and that public investment is fully financed by loans. We shall now consider the repercussions of financing government investment partly or fully by taxation. It is easy to show that the amount of saving corresponding to a given level of investment (private and public) will be reduced by the amount of additional taxation. Indeed, our equation of the demand for and supply of consumption goods can now be written, if we abstract from capital imports, as follows:

$$C_1 + T = T_2 + T'_2 + S_2 \qquad (11)$$

where T'_2 are the additional taxes raised in Department II, or

$$C_1 + T_1 = T'_2 + S_2 \qquad (12)$$

because T (I) is the total tax covering the administrative expenditure and T_1 and T_2 are its parts raised in Departments I and II, respectively. Let us now add $T'_1 + S_1$ on both sides, where T'_1 is part of the additional tax raised in Department I

$$C_1 + T_1 + T'_1 + S_1 = T'_1 + T'_2 + S_1 + S_2. \qquad (13)$$

The left-hand side is nothing but the value of the production of Department I or private and public investment (I). The right-hand side is equal to T', i.e. the total additional tax plus S, the total saving

$$I = T' + S. \qquad (14)$$

It is easy to show that if capital imports (F) are taken into consideration equation 14 will change to

$$I = T' + S + F. \tag{15}$$

It can be seen from equation 15 that investment will always generate the saving necessary to finance it in excess of taxation and imports of capital.

Although taxation reduces the amount of saving which is generated by a given level of investment, this will not necessarily mean a reduction in pressure on real wages. (We have already dealt with a similar problem when discussing the consequences of an increase in the balanced administrative budget.) Direct taxation on lower income groups, or indirect taxes, will, of course, mean a reduction in real wages. As to taxes on capitalists, they will be met only in part by a reduction in their consumption, while in part they will be paid at the expense of their savings. In the latter case, there is only a shift from savings to taxes, without any change in prices.

Nevertheless, the reduction of capitalists' consumption achieved by taxation of profits will help by *mitigating* inflationary pressures. It is true that no essential commodities will be released in this way. The capitalists will not eat less under the impact of taxation. But, as a result, to a given level of investment there will correspond a lower level of industrial employment, because less will be produced for capitalists' consumption, and this will reduce the inflationary pressures caused by rapid development. Moreover, in the longer run this policy will help to shape the development in the direction of the expansion of essential industries. It is true that this can be achieved through enforcing an appropriate investment plan by direct means, e.g. licensing of investment, but it is clear that without a parallel tax policy this might involve considerable difficulties. Indeed, prices of non-essential consumer goods would increase under the pressure of demand and thus create a strong tendency for investment in the respective industries, which it might be difficult to control.

The reduction of capitalists' consumption will also be beneficial from the point of view of the balance of payments, because it will reduce the demand for imported luxuries. It is true that import restrictions can cope with this problem, but here again the reduction of demand for such imports will facilitate the enforcement of restrictions.

In addition to limiting capitalists' consumption, financing public investment by taxation presents still another advantage. It reduces the creation of liquid assets. This may be unimportant if there is no tendency towards inflation. If, however, as a result of an inadequate supply of consumption goods, an inflationary spiral has been in existence for some time, the large amount of liquid assets will stimulate speculative hoarding and thus will help to aggravate the primary inflationary process.[8]

In the light of the above, financing public investment by taxation of profits appears to be a sound policy. It should be noticed that in this way only such profits would be taxed away as are in fact created by public investment. Indeed, if taxation in excess of the administrative budget is exactly equal to public investment, equation 15 will become

$$I_{pr} = S + F \qquad (16)$$

where I_{pr} stands for private investment. For if we subtract T' from equation 15 we obtain on the left-hand side private investment (I_{pr}), because we assume that public investment is equal to T'. It follows that if public investment is fully financed by taxation, the savings and profits generated are such as would be obtained if there were no public investment.[9] Thus an increase in public investment accompanied by a correspondingly higher revenue from taxation of profits would not have an adverse effect on incentives to private investment.

The above puts the role of financing of public investment by taxation of profits into proper perspective. This taxation will prevent public investment from increasing profits and capitalists' consumption. There will remain, however, the effect of higher investment upon the demand of workers for consumption goods.

It follows that, while balancing public investment by taxation of profits appears to be a sound policy, it will not fully 'neutralise' the inflationary impact of such investment. It may be shown that such monetary measures as banking restrictions are also inadequate for dealing with the problem of inflation resulting from a high level of investment.

Let us consider the significance of banking credit restrictions as anti-inflationary measures. The main anti-inflationary influence of credit restrictions is obviously exerted through depressing the level of investment. Now the reduction of investment in fixed capital will obviously upset the pace of development. Thus inflationary pressure resulting from rapid development would be cured by slowing it down. If this is deemed necessary, however, it may be done by the more direct means of either reducing public investment or licensing private investment. The latter will help to reduce private investment on a selective basis. Selective restrictions of long-term bank credit for financing private investment may, of course, be used for the same purpose. This, however, would not exclude inessential investment financed from the firm's profits.

There still remains the effect of credit restrictions upon investment in inventories. However, as long as there is no tendency for hoarding, only limited reductions in investment in inventories can be achieved without hampering the expansion of production.

We may conclude that credit restrictions can play an important anti-inflationary role only when directed against hoarding of commodites, which is a secondary effect of already advanced inflation. When applied in such a case they must be on a highly selective basis so as not to impede the process of development itself.

Such a system, however, may be rather difficult to operate. A credit given for an essential purpose may frequently be used, at least indirectly, for speculative hoarding: indeed, such a credit may release the firm's own funds and thus make them available for speculative activity. The system of selective credit restrictions may have to be very complicated in order to be run effectively. For this reason another way of combating tendencies for hoarding commodites may be preferable if an inflationary spiral is in existence. This system was applied for the first time, and with success, in the Chinese People's Republic, to put a stop to the hyper-inflation which was inherited from the previous regime. It consists of maintaining the real value of deposits, government bonds and banking credits by revaluing them continuously according to established price indices. This prevents a tendency to convert money and other liquid assets into commodities, and at the same time discourages borrowing for speculative purposes.[10]

Neither this method nor selective credit restrictions, can, of course, cope with what we described as 'primary' inflation. Their only purpose is to prevent the aggravation of this primary inflation by speculative hoarding. The primary inflationary pressure experienced in the course of rapid economic development is, as shown above, the result of basic disproportions in productive relations. Thus these pressures cannot be prevented by purely financial devices. The solution of the problem must be based on economic policies embracing the whole process of development.

NOTES AND REFERENCES

1. This does not involve an assumption that the indebtedness of small proprietors does not increase, because such an increase may occur as a result of *investment* financed by credit.
2. It should be noted that despite the small volume of capital equipment in relation to labour force in underdeveloped countries, such equipment as exists is frequently underutilised.
3. It should not be concluded that financing public investment by loans is particularly desirable. We shall argue at a later stage that financing of public investment by taxes on profits is preferable because it helps to reduce inflationary pressures.
4. This does not exclude the possibility of a quick expansion of agriculture in underdeveloped countries if the institutional obstacles are eliminated.
5. It should be noted that after the problem of rigidity of the supply of food has been overcome, the problem of supply of industrial consumer goods usually becomes more acute. Indeed, if the rise in food prices involves a shift in distribution of income towards big landowners, money lenders or merchants, the prevention of such a price rise will tend to increase the demand for industrial mass consumption goods. This is a special case of an economic law: the elimination of scarcity prices in one sector, through a higher supply, increases the probability of the appearance of scarcity prices in another sector.
6. Unless this benefits only rural capitalists.
7. It should be perhaps noted that the policies of reducing, or eliminating, dividend transfers cannot always be considered as being aimed solely at immediate improvement of the balance of payments. In many instances, these policies may be mainly a manifestation of the battle of an underdeveloped country against the political in-

fluence of foreign companies. The retaliation of these companies by manoeuvres to reduce exports of the products concerned may even temporarily lead to the weakening of the balance of payments position. Such will be the case especially when one or a few companies play a dominant role in the foreign trade of the country involved.

8. The reduction in the creation of liquid assets will also facilitate the control of the structure of investment by direct means, e.g. licensing.

9. It should be noted that if public investment is increased considerably over a short period, the rise in taxes on profits necessary to finance it is likely to be less than the increment in public investment, unless other taxes are reduced. Indeed, the resulting upswing in economic activity will raise the revenue from 'old' taxes while the administrative budget is not likely to expand much in a short period. Thus a part of the increase in public investment will automatically be covered by tax revenue.

10. It should be noted that the application of this measure would cause a fall in the values of private securities which would not be 'insured' against the rise in prices. This feature is in fact common to all monetary measures against the hoarding of commodities. In fact, credit restrictions would cause a fall in the values of both government and private securities.

6

Forms of
Foreign Aid:
*An Economic Analysis**

❀

INTRODUCTION

Few topics are the object of a more voluminous literature than
foreign aid. And yet the very concept of foreign aid needs clari-
fication.[1] This will be the main purpose of the present paper,
which, at the same time, will review the principal forms of
economic aid and evaluate them.

The paper is in three parts. The first deals with the impact of
foreign aid on economic development. The second reviews the
different modalities of economic aid. The third discusses the
problem of aid through trade.

The present paper makes use of contributions and reviews of
literature prepared by the following authors, to whom go our
thanks: I. Blaszczyszyn, J. Kotowicz, T. Kozak, M. Paszynski,
C. Prawdzic, W. Rydygier.

FOREIGN AID AND ECONOMIC DEVELOPMENT

Definition of Economic Aid
From the point of view of the recipient country foreign economic aid occurs when:

(*a*) The country receives additional resources in foreign currency, or its equivalent in goods, over the capacity to import

* Abridged version of a paper written with Ignacy Sachs for the European
Coordination Centre for Research and Documentation in the Social Sciences
(Vienna) in connection with a research project on comparative forms of
assistance to countries undergoing development. First published in *Social
Science Information*, 1966, (1), 21–44.

generated by exports or financed from accumulated reserves, without the need of immediate repayment and at a cost lower than the prevailing rates of commercial loans.

(*b*) These additional resources are used in order to improve the recipient country's economic performance above the level otherwise attainable, that is either the country achieves a higher rate of growth without reducing the anticipated consumption of working people or it implements the anticipated rate of growth, managing to increase the volume of popular consumption over the anticipated level. (A combination of the two situations described above is, of course, possible.)

We assume that this higher rate of growth implies changes in the structure of the economy, although in the short run structural rigidities or imbalances which give rise to scarcities in supplies of determined commodities and services can only be relieved by additional imports.[2]

The country's economic performance is not improved, however, when additional resources are used to increase the consumption of 'luxuries', i.e. to permit the implementation of the anticipated rate of growth with an unchanged level of popular consumption and a lower volume of internal savings.

This is why we cannot equate all the inflows of foreign capital with foreign aid.[3] Whether it should be considered as 'aid', or not, depends, on the one hand, on the comparative cost of such capital and, on the other, on the use made of it by the recipient country, which may not always have a free hand to act without taking into consideration the suggestions of the donor. Thus a certain measure of arbitrariness cannot be entirely dissociated from evaluations of the foreign aid received.

We should discard as fallacious all ideas of assisting a country by putting at its disposal an amount of accumulated local currency, as long as it remains unconvertible. Two situations may occur. Either the country concerned has no free productive capacity and, in this case, the additional demand generated by releasing accumulated local funds will lead to inflationary pressures. Or free capacity does exist and then the financing of additional production by having recourse to deficit financing has the same effect as that of financing it by foreign loans in local currency.

Turning now to the definition of aid from the point of view of the donor country, we should make a clear distinction between two positions.

(*a*) The donor country has no free productive capacity (as usually happens in socialist countries).

(*b*) The donor country does not fully use its productive capacity, because of lack of effective demand (a frequent situation in developed capitalist countries).

In the former case, giving foreign aid, embodied in an export surplus, means a sacrifice because the aggregate internal expenditure (i.e. national income less exports plus imports) will be less than the income generated, which cannot be stepped up above the maximum level warranted by the productive capacity. Were there no export surplus, the aggregate internal expenditure would be equal to the income generated at the maximum level.

In the latter case, the picture changes entirely: the export surplus, similar to investment, has a 'multiplier' effect, so that the aggregate domestic expenditure after deduction of the export surplus from the income thus generated is higher than the income which would be generated without the export surplus. We may say, therefore, that by giving economic aid to other countries a developed country with free productive capacity assists its own economy in obtaining a higher level of economic activity. Foreign aid, far from being a burden on it, can perform a very useful role in achieving full employment while it serves a better purpose than encouraging the armaments' race, provided it does not compete with public expenditures, other than armaments, which are of considerable importance for the country in question.[4]

Criteria of Evaluation of Foreign Aid

From the definition established above, it follows that:

(*a*) Foreign aid means essentially an improvement of external conditions of growth;

(*b*) Its evaluation depends essentially on the full knowledge of the general problems of economic development of the recipient country.

We can measure with some precision the extent to which a given volume of foreign aid, provided on certain conditions, increases the recipient country's capacity to import in the short run and how it will adversely affect the future position of the balance of payments through the servicing of the debt and the repayment of the principal.

From the quantitative point of view foreign aid can be compared to a positive shift in terms of trade to the extent to which both increase the capacity to import of the country without any effort on its part. But foreign credits must be repaid. Moreover, a positive shift in terms of trade has a continuous effect, comparable, strictly speaking, to a continuous flow of foreign assistance. It will be easily seen, therefore, that an adverse shift in terms of trade cancels the effects of the inflow of foreign aid and, what is more, must be compensated by a continuous inflow of that aid as long as the worsened terms of trade do not improve. In such circumstances a perfectly legitimate procedure consists in subtracting from the net inflow of capital[5] the 'losses' suffered on account of adverse terms of trade, even though such an operation involves a somewhat arbitrary choice of the initial level of export and import prices considered for the purpose of the calculation as fair. Data collected by different UN agencies point to the rather disturbing fact that the 'real' inflow of long-term capital to the developing countries in the last decade was to a great extent offset by the growing burden of servicing foreign debt and the losses motivated by the adverse shifts in the terms of trade. Without going into the details of the matter, which will be dealt with below, we should like to emphasise even at this stage of the argument that a positive shift in the terms of trade of developing countries or a reduction in the volume of the transfer of profits arising from direct foreign investment would improve the external conditions of their growth in just the same way as a flow of foreign aid of the same volume, with the difference, however, that no increase in foreign indebtedness would occur.[6]

Turning now to the second aspect of the problem, mentioned at the beginning of this section, we shall examine at some length the role of foreign trade in the process of economic development of an underdeveloped country.

All the tensions and bottlenecks of such an economy can be translated into additional demand for imports. This demand arises with regard to the products of the 'supply-determined' industries which cannot push their volume of production beyond a certain level,[7] and must be paid for by export surpluses produced by 'demand-determined' industries. The higher the postulated rate of growth, the greater will be the necessary volume of imports. To pay for them it will be necessary to resort to less and less 'effective' exports[8] and to introduce more and more capital-intensive exports,[9] up to the point where the advantages arising from a higher volume of foreign trade will be offset by the disadvantages resulting from the increase of the capital-output ratio.

From these considerations, we see that an inflow of foreign aid may be instrumental in stepping up the rate of growth of an economy faced by the barrier of foreign trade. But such a result by no means follows automatically from the inflow of foreign aid, which may be dissipated in additional consumption of 'luxuries'.

We may look at the matter from yet another angle. Given an initial economic structure we may construct, on the basis of an assumed income distribution and of a postulated rate of growth, a plan anticipating the trend of demands for necessities, luxuries, capital goods and intermediate goods the inputs of which are necessary for the production of final goods. These demands will be met partly by domestic production, and the rest will have to be imported. In principle, the necessary imports can always be covered by production for export. But the feasible structure of this production may not fit the conditions prevailing in the foreign markets. The country is thus faced with a deficit in foreign trade and the nonutilisation, to the same extent, of its productive capacity. In such a situation of sectoral imbalances between supply and demand, after having taken full advantage of all the possibilities of foreign trade, the possibility of taking foreign aid to the tune of the potential import surplus might be considered.

But such an inflow of foreign assistance automatically adds to the financial resources of the country, which permits increasing investment without reducing consumption, or *vice versa*, without risking inflationary pressures. Thus in evaluating foreign aid we should see clearly its double function.

Two questions, therefore, should be asked here:

(*a*) To what extent has the inflow of foreign aid improved the country's balance of payments position; and has this improvement been used to remove the bottlenecks in the supply of capital goods, necessities, luxuries or intermediate goods?

(*b*) Were the additional financial resources instrumental in raising the rate of growth by increasing investment over the level of domestic savings or releasing local savings for consumption; and, if so, did they finance an increase in the consumption of necessities, of luxuries or materialise in a higher volume of social services?

Aid may be considered appropriately utilised if:

(i) it adds, *ceteris paribus*, to investments other than those increasing the output of luxuries; or

(ii) it adds, *ceteris paribus*, to the consumption of 'essentials' and/or the output of social services.

But aid defeats its own purpose when it releases local savings for additional consumption of luxuries by foregoing the taxation of higher income groups and/or non-essentials, or fosters investment leading to an increased output of luxuries.[10] Such investment merely adds to the lop-sidedness of the economy, and leads to 'perverse growth': in the short run it promotes growth, but in the long run it adversely affects the growth prospects of the economy. For it ties up capital goods, intermediate goods and essentials, which otherwise would have been used to expand productive capacity and employment in the sectors of the economy which turn out essentials, capital goods and intermediate goods.

Thus the role played by foreign aid can be evaluated only in the context of a comprehensive analysis of the development problems of the recipient country seen as a whole. Such an analysis requires the framing of a plan and, therefore, comprehensive planning should be considered as a prerequisite of any action aimed at a rational utilisation of available foreign aid.[11]

Before going into a more detailed examination of some aspects of the impact of foreign aid on the economy of the recipient country, we should like to stress that of the two functions of foreign aid, the one pertaining to the realm of foreign trade is by far the more important, contrary to some entrenched prejudices.

For quite a time many economists believed that foreign trade would never become a bottleneck, while in a poor country the barrier of insufficient accumulation would put a low ceiling on the rate of growth. Yet, by means of appropriate taxation and other institutional measures, the relative share of investment in the national income of developing countries can be greatly increased without affecting the consumption of working people. However, the majority of developing countries must struggle against the obstacle of an inadequate and inelastic world demand for their feasible exports.[12]

The foreign currency gap is, therefore, likely to be retained in practice for the evaluation of needs in foreign aid, although from a purely technical point of view, the planner should perform two independent calculations: of the foreign trade currency gap and of the savings gap arising at a postulated rate of growth and the rate of investment required to implement it. Where the savings gap is higher than the foreign currency gap, it should be reduced to the level of the foreign currency gap by measures of taxation purporting the reduction of non-essential consumption. Failing this, it would be necessary to increase the foreign currency gap up to the level of the savings gap.

The Impact of Foreign Aid

It is sometimes believed that the evaluation of foreign aid can be inferred from the commodity pattern of the additional imports financed by such aid.

This, however, is absolutely wrong. Additional imports of equipment may prove detrimental, if they are earmarked for the expansion of productive capacity in the industries turning out luxuries, while additional imports of necessities, by helping to close the gap between supply and effective demand, may, in fact, permit a stepping up of the level of investment without the danger of inducing inflation. Also, credits tied to the purchase of specified sorts of goods should not be rejected by the recipient country, as long as those goods belong to the actual list of preferential imports. Obviously, foreign currency which otherwise would have been spent on the purchase of these goods

is being released for other destinations. In such a way, shipments of grain on credit—if imports of grain cannot be prevented—may amount to an indirect financing of purchases of
equipment.

We may turn now to a more complex instance of dislocation,
when the final impact of the foreign aid is by no means apparent.
Let us suppose that instead of building a machine industry,
which is technically feasible, a country chooses to spend the
same funds on a motor-car factory. It will subsequently use the
available foreign aid to import machines of the highest priority,
which will, in fact, amount to financing the superfluous motor-
car industry. To make our example still more convincing, we
may imagine that our automobile industry can produce trucks
or passenger cars, the former having a high social priority and
the latter a very low one. Without foreign aid, the factory would
have a programme of production of trucks. But foreign aid
becomes available and is utilised for imports of trucks, while the
local factory specialises in passenger cars. Nobody would question the necessity of putting new trucks in service. But under the
circumstances, aid coming in the form of trucks is, in reality,
used to finance the production of passenger motor-cars.

The substance of our argument is, therefore, the following:
we should always look at the final impact of foreign aid, following step by step all the successive dislocations caused by the
additional imports financed through foreign aid. Aid will be
efficient to the extent to which it closes gaps between effective
demand and supply in the process of the development of the
recipient country.

The Absorptive Capacity[13]

How much aid can a country take? On a purely theoretical
plane, any amount of economic aid can be swallowed, as an
inflow of foreign capital will always increase the volume of
aggregate domestic expenditure and, whenever properly used
in accordance with a plan, will materialise also in a higher rate
of growth of the national income. But the higher this rate, the
higher will have to be the relative share of imports in the increment of the national income, because of the lack of free productive capacities, including the skilled labour force, which we

consider for the moment to be an importable item. In other words, the 'effectiveness' of the foreign aid measured by the marginal ratio of the increment of the national income to the additional imports will tend to 0, while the ratio of the increment of the aggregate expenditure to the additional imports will tend to 1.[14]

Before we reach this limit, however, two other factors are likely to set a ceiling to the absorptive capacity of the recipient country.

On the one hand, there is the problem of financial capacity to service the debt. The better the terms of credit, of course, the less will be the burden of servicing a given volume of credits. But unless new outlets for exports are created,[15] servicing of the debt is likely to become a problem if the country indulges in taking credits for some years.

An increasing share of foreign currency earned through exports will be devoted to this aim and the net capacity to import will, in consequence, decrease, unless new credits are taken. This will start a snowball process, which only shows that even sustained foreign assistance will not solve the problems of the developing countries as long as the stalemate in foreign trade persists. We must never lose sight of the fact that credits are but a form of postponing the payment for a delivery of goods; ultimately this payment will have normally to take the form of an export.

On the other hand, the capacity to absorb foreign aid depends to a great extent on the country's availability of skilled manpower of different grades and types. Obviously our previous assumption, made at the beginning of this section, that skilled labour could always be imported from abroad is unrealistic. At best a developing country can rely for some time on highly qualified foreign technicians, but already the medium grades required in great numbers cannot be brought from abroad due to both difficulties in recruitment and the political complications that are likely to arise. That is why technical assistance and the so-called 'investment in human resources' should be considered as the complement of economic foreign aid in the form of credits for the purchase of goods. The volume and forms of such assistance must be carefully harmonized with the economic development plan. Normally, contracts for the supply of complete industrial plants should contain clauses about technical assistance. But the problem is, of course, broader.[16]

PRINCIPAL FORMS OF ECONOMIC AID

Before we pass in review the different modalities of economic aid—grants, credits, grain loans, direct investments—we should like to comment on two general aspects of all such types of aid, namely:

(*a*) Their relationship with the public and the private sectors both in the donor and in the recipient countries.

(*b*) The pros and cons of bi- and multi-lateral arrangements.

As far as the first issue is concerned, the developing countries have good reasons to prefer aid coming from public funds and put at the disposal of the recipient country's government. Such aid eliminates, or at least reduces, possible pressures on the part of powerful private corporations of the donor countries, operating in the recipient countries. At the other end, it makes easier the proper utilisation of available foreign assistance in harmony with the economic plan objectives. The least we can say is that it is always possible for the authorities of the recipient country to make use of the foreign aid received in such a way as to strengthen the private sector, if it chooses to do so, while the contrary is not true. It is difficult to imagine that a private concern in the recipient country will avail itself of foreign loans put at its disposal for any other purpose than that of expanding its own productive capacity, however low might be the social priority attached to such a project. The individual interests of firms cannot, of course, be taken as identical with the social priorities established in the plan, unless we believe that the market mechanism allocates investment in the best way. The whole experience of the developing countries belies such a belief; were we to go by market indications alone, we should have a completely lop-sided development, with a hypertrophy of the sector turning out luxuries. At any rate, planning would have to be considered as perfectly redundant. Actually, making foreign loans available to specified private firms amounts in some cases to influencing the pattern of investment in the recipient country by the donor institution.

Besides, several developing countries are interested in expanding their public sector, as an objective of their economic and social policies, aimed at strengthening their independence and speeding up the necessary structural transformations.

While asking for an increased stream of aid coming from public funds and going to the public sector, many economists and politicians at the same time advance unexceptionable arguments in favour of multi-lateral aid, channelled through the United Nations and their specialised agencies, rather than offered through bi-lateral government-to-government contacts. Such a shift towards a system of multi-lateral international aid distribution would, in their opinion, reduce to a minimum the political aspects of aid giving.[17] They might be right, although not quite in touch with the complex realities of the present world political scene.[18] Whatever the opinions expressed on this subject, we must be prepared to work in the immediate future mainly in terms of bi-lateral economic relations.

We are convinced, furthermore, that bi-lateral assistance has something to recommend it: it does not require very heavy machinery, it can adjust itself to new and elastic forms and it can be more easily coordinated and harmonized with trade relations, at least between countries adopting some measure of long term planning. In this context, we should like once more to stress the necessity of thinking simultaneously in terms of trade and aid.

Grants (*Gifts*)

From the strictly economic point of view, a free grant is, of course, the best form of foreign aid. Aggregate internal expenditure exceeds the income generated by the total of the grant and no repayment is involved, either at the moment or in the future. But economic aid has been too much of an instrument of policy, not to have some strings or second thoughts attached in many actual cases of free grants (with the exception of rather minor contributions, made on a humanitarian basis, to assist countries affected by some natural calamity, to feed destitute children or to help victims of war and refugees).

This is why grants cannot be judged just on their face economic value. But neither can any precise measure be given of the political price attached to them.

Credits

Loans given on terms better than the currently prevailing ones in standard commercial transactions, usually tied to specific investment projects and associated with some form of technical assistance, constitute the bulk of what is termed 'foreign economic aid' given to the developing countries. The borderline between the 'commercial' loans and 'long term' loans is, of course, rather arbitrary and, rigorously speaking, aid should be computed as the difference between the actual cost of credit borne by the recipient country and the cost-to-be of a standard commercial credit. Such an approach would lead, however, to endless complications of a purely technical nature, and make our quantitative estimates of foreign aid still more shaky. The more so, because the terms of credits granted to developing countries have recently been changing quite substantially, not to speak of the differences attached to the kind of supplies which are offered on deferred payment basis, so that it would be quite difficult to define for reference the 'standard commercial loan'. (The recent downward trend in the cost of foreign credits can, to a great extent, be ascribed to the action of the Soviet Union and other socialist countries, which not only broke the Western monopoly for the supply of industrial equipment to the former colonial and dependent countries, but introduced and generalised the practice of loans, repayable in 10 to 12 years and bearing a low rate of interest of no more than 2·5 per cent. Even if the conditions offered by the socialist countries are from time to time overbidden now, we should not forget that before the emergence of the socialist countries on the world market for industrial equipment, the developing countries had to content themselves with much less favourable conditions of deferred payment.[19])

Moreover, the whole approach of this paper is that of not separating foreign aid from trade. We suggest, therefore, that credits should be classified by ranging them from expensive commercial loans to 'soft' credits repayable in local currency, over such a length of time that they approach asymptotically the category of grants.

Apart from the distinction, already discussed in general

terms, between public and private loans, we can classify the different types of credits available to the developing countries according to the cost of servicing (including the repayment of the principal) and the modalities of such repayment.

The cost of servicing depends on three elements: the grace period, the length of the credit and the rate of interest. The average yearly burden decreases with the length both of the grace period and of the credit itself and increases with the level of the rate of interest. It is more sensitive to the first two elements than to the third one.

Of course, the less the cost of servicing the loan the better the loan is, from the point of view of the recipient country, subject to the note of caution already expressed about grants: the more 'commercial' a loan the less likely it is to have political strings attached.

In our opinion, in the evaluation of a loan the stipulations about the method of its repayment are just as important as its 'cost'. Broadly speaking, we can distinguish three modalities:

(*a*) Repayment in hard (convertible) currency;

(*b*) Repayment in local, unconvertible currency of the recipient country (soft loans);

(*c*) Repayment in goods.

In the first case, the recipient country must increase its income from exports in order to earn the necessary hard currency to service the debt, or be prepared to reduce its potential imports to the same amount. Otherwise, it will have to seek new loans to consolidate its foreign debt. At the risk of being repetitive, let us stress that a loan does not solve the problems of foreign trade, but merely postpones them. Without a lasting solution in the sphere of foreign trade, the only economically— but by no means politically—viable alternative is that of a continuous inflow of grants!

In the second case, the recipient country's situation is somewhat better, because the creditor country becomes interested in finding in the recipient country new exportable goods, to be purchased with the local currency received in repayment of the credit. But two dangers always loom: that of financing from these funds part of 'normal' imports, which otherwise would have been paid for in hard currency, or that of accumulating a huge sum in local currency, which either will finally have to be converted (we then fall back on the first case) or may be used as an instrument of interference in the economic life of the recipient country.

The soundest from the point of view of the recipient country is the third modality, especially if repayment in goods is negotiated in addition to the 'normal' volume of trade between the countries concerned, or, at least, constitutes part of the foreseen increment in trade relations between the two partners. If equipment for a plant is being furnished on a deferred payment basis and the credit is going to be cancelled out by shipments of part of the output of the new plant, we are in the presence of a truly 'self-liquidating' and mutually advantageous credit. Different variations of the pattern described above have been suggested, from the Indonesian 'production sharing' formula to the industrial branch agreements (discussed below in *Aid through Trade*), which combine elements of loans and of long term trade arrangements. These arrangements do not necessarily involve payments in terms of products of a given plant, but may be based on equivalent future exports of other goods. In our opinion, relatively cheap loans repayable in goods are the most viable form of aid to developing countries. For they combine, to the mutual interest of the recipient and donor countries, elements of assistance and trade and contribute to a lasting solution of the problem of insufficient export outlets at present affecting so many developing countries. The current practice in this respect, already existing between some socialist and developing countries, should be considerably expanded and equally extended to the sphere of economic relations between the developing and the capitalist developed countries.

Grain Loans
A substantial part of American aid to the developing countries takes the form of supplies of grain under the provision of US Public Law 480. This is a highly complex form, combining elements of trade, loan and grant. An attempt to analyse its different aspects follows.[20]

From the point of view of the donor country, i.e. USA, the whole operation consists of shipping abroad a part of the agricultural surpluses, which are anyhow purchased by the Commodity Credit Corporation as part of the policies of support to agricultural incomes. That is why, strictly speaking, no cost whatever is involved on the side of the donor country.

PL 480 established four titles under which grain surpluses are delivered to foreign countries, as well as some general conditions, such as the obligation of transporting at least 50 per cent of the grain by ships under the American flag, the necessity of making some additional cash purchases of American agricultural products, the acceptance of the clause forbidding competition with American agricultural goods in third markets, etc. The most important is Title I, with which we shall deal below in more detail. As for Titles II and III, they relate to operations of relief, charity and barter transactions. Title IV relates to long-term loans, repayable in dollars, with an additional clause giving the USA some control over the use of the proceeds of the sale of grain in local currency by the government of the recipient country.

Title I—as mentioned above, by far the most important—technically deals with cash sales of grain against local unconvertible currency, which are credited to a special account of the donor country, thus creating the so-called 'counterpart funds',[21] but at the same time establishes directly, or by supplementary bi-lateral agreements, an elaborate mechanism for the utilisation of the counterpart funds. Part of these funds serves to finance the expenditure of American agencies in the recipient country. Another share is earmarked for loans granted to American private companies operating in the recipient country or local enterprises affiliated to them (the so-called 'Cooley loans'). The rest of the counterpart funds is usually lent or granted by the USA to the government of the recipient country for projects mutually agreed upon. In other words, to the extent to which the counterpart funds finance American activities, this is tantamount to a transfer of funds, which otherwise would have taken the form of transfers of dollars. Similarly, the Cooley loans take the place of an inflow of foreign capital to a particular section of the private sector.

To the extent of this utilisation of counterpart funds, PL 480 amounts to replacing certain dollar flows from the donor to the recipient countries by shipment of grain and, therefore, no foreign aid whatever is involved. Roughly speaking one-third of the value of shipments of grain to the developing countries from 1954 till the end of 1964 should be deducted to allow for these transfers (including the Cooley loans). Let us turn now to the remaining two-thirds.

The grain supplies, which in fact are nothing but grants, have the same double effect as imports of capital in general. On the one hand, they supply the deficient necessities and thus permit the country concerned to develop at a higher rate without inflationary pressures, or counteract existing inflation.

On the other hand, they ease the problem of financing investment, because the proceeds from the sales of grain provide a source of this financing.

As to the release of the counterpart funds for loans and grants for development (excluding the Cooley loans), this has, like all loans in local currency (see *Definition of Foreign Aid*), an effect fully equivalent to deficit financing. Thus, such releases do not constitute any real assistance in financing government investment and must not affect its total volume, determined by the considerations of full utilisation of resources without creating inflationary pressures. If, however, the donor country is reluctant to permit the blockage of counterpart funds and insists on playing the game of releasing them for projects mutually agreed upon, and further supplies of grain, depending on the 'utilisation' of the counterpart funds, this creates a channel for the donor country's influence upon public investment in the recipient country. This effect will grow in importance very quickly unless shipments of grain under Title IV become the dominant form of exports of American agricultural surpluses.

The imponderabilia attached to this situation might be of such a nature as to make it preferable to the developing countries to avail themselves of Title IV rather than of Title I, even though the imponderabilia will not be entirely eliminated in this way[22] and the necessity of servicing the debt in hard currency will have to be faced.

Of course a still better solution would consist in convincing the American government that an accumulation of counterpart funds should not be considered as an obstacle to further supplies of grain under PL 480. Such accumulation could be viewed as a transfer of funds to finance the future activities of American agencies in the recipient country after the deliveries of grain under PL 480 come to an end.

The above is not meant as denying the positive effect of the supplies of grain in question, apart from the handling of the counterpart funds. However, even with regard to the positive impact of grain deliveries, care should be taken to avoid two negative side effects: a mood of complacency towards the problem of agricultural backwardness on the part of the ruling classes in the recipient country and the temptation to sell the available additional grain supplies at low prices, in order to gain popularity among the urban population, with no regard to the fact that such a policy may discourage local agricultural producers and compel them to reduce the area under food crops. Recent experience of several developing countries shows that both dangers are real.

Foreign Direct Investment

The widespread practice of including the inflow of foreign direct private investment in the category of 'aid' can be explained, though not justified, on two grounds: it results from the application of a purely technical criterion, by which all inflows of long-term capital are considered as aid with no regard to their cost and purpose, and/or from the doctrinal position that investment of foreign private capital is by definition sound and necessary to the recipient economy, because it passes through the test of market, the only reliable guide to orient the allocation of investment.[23]

Enough has been said already in this paper to discard these two criteria as irrelevant. But a few other misconceptions about direct foreign investment should still be dispelled.

It is sometimes argued that direct foreign investment is cheaper to the recipient country than any credit because it need not be repaid. Even if we assume that foreign capital will not be repatriated at any moment, the argument is based on a sophism: it is true that on the 'capital account' the inflow of foreign direct investment will never be offset under such an assumption by an outflow of repatriated capital. But the profits transferred abroad may exceed the cost of servicing a foreign loan,[24] while the reinvested profits add to the book value of foreign investment with no further inflow of foreign capital (at best they can be said to diminish the outflow of profits). Profits earned by foreign investors from these reploughed profits will again be transferred, at least partly, abroad. We are thus in the presence of an endless snowballing process, as contrasted with a loan which creates obligations for a definite number of years. It may be easily shown that in the long run the impact of continuous foreign direct investment on the balance of payments of the recipient country must be negative (we do not discuss here the indirect consequences in the form of additional exports or import substitution, which would be the same whatever the form of financing the new plant), unless the inflow of foreign investment grows substantially from year to year.[25]

To illustrate our argument, we may well imagine that a country seeks a net inflow of 100 units of foreign capital per year. This capital yields profits, starting from the end of the year of the inflow, of 15 per cent *per annum*, of which 10 per cent are transferred abroad and 5 per cent reinvested. We want to ascertain what should be the inflow of foreign investment.

Table 1 gives the results of the exercise performed for six years.

TABLE 1

Year	Gross inflow of capital	Foreign investment at the beginning of the year	Foreign investment at the end of the year	Profits transferred abroad	Net inflow of capital
1	111·1	111·1	116·7	11·1	100
2	124·1	240·8	252·8	24·1	100
3	139·2	392·0	411·6	39·2	100
4	156·9	568·5	596·9	56·9	100
5	177·4	774·3	813·0	77·4	100
6	201·4	1014·4	1065·1	101·4	100
	910·1			310·1	600

We see that by the sixth year the ratio of gross inflow to net inflow exceeds 2:1.

Table 2 performs the same exercise on the assumption that two-thirds of annual profits are reinvested and only one-third transferred abroad.

TABLE 2

Year	Gross inflow of capital	Foreign investment at the beginning of the year	Foreign investment at the end of the year	Profits transferred abroad	Net inflow of capital
1	105·3	105·3	115·8	5·3	100
2	111·4	227·2	249·9	11·4	100
3	118·4	368·3	405·1	18·4	100
4	126·6	531·7	584·9	26·6	100
5	136	720·9	793	36	100
6	146·9	939·9	1033·9	46·9	100
	744·6			144·6	600

The results are somewhat better for the recipient country, but the trend is the same; in the sixth year the ratio of gross inflow to net inflow is already 1·47:1. The results of the two operations for the six-year period are compared in Table 3.[26]

TABLE 3

	Case A	Case B
Book value of foreign investment as percentage of the gross inflow of foreign capital	117·4%	138·8%
Book value of foreign investment as percentage of the net inflow of foreign capital	177·5%	172·3%
Profits transferred abroad as percentage of the gross inflow of foreign capital for the whole period under consideration	34%	19·4%
Profits transferred abroad as percentage of the net inflow of foreign capital for the whole period under consideration	51·7%	24·1%

Even if there were no other arguments beyond that of the long-term worsening of the balance of payments the case for private foreign investment would be very weak. There are obviously no prospects of setting in motion a continuously growing stream of direct foreign investment in the developing countries, not to speak of the political inconvenience of having a big foreign private sector, likely to act as a powerful pressure group.

And let us not forget that we took a conservative figure for the average rate of profit. It is, in fact, not unexpected that from the recipient country's point of view private foreign investment should prove more costly than the majority of commercial loans. After all, by its very nature and avowed purpose it is guided by the profit motive. Normally, foreign investors will not put their money in a developing country unless they expect a rate of profit not lower than in their own country, plus a substantial risk premium; the more independent and progressive a country, the higher this premium will be.[27]

There are, of course, instances of huge foreign direct investment, motivated not so much by the immediate profit expectation as by the desire to control sources of oil, minerals and other raw materials, although in the case of oil the two motives usually coincide.[28]

The crucial importance of oil royalties for the budgets of several developing countries should not make us oblivious of the fact that a considerable proportion of very high profits is still being transferred abroad in spite of some progress in the redistribution of income from oil production achieved by a few developing countries in recent years. And there are still the dangers to which a country becomes exposed when it depends to such a degree on a mono-export controlled by powerful foreign firms involved in worldwide operations, which may prompt them at any time to take decisions affecting the whole future of the recipient country (e.g., to reduce the output in one place in order to put into operation a new field in another country). At any rate one fails to see how these situations could be brought under the heading of 'foreign aid', even in the most remote manner.

One more argument frequently invoked by the partisans of direct foreign investment is that it brings the necessary know-how to the developing country. The fact is beyond dispute; but in most cases this know-how could be purchased at even cheaper rates on a commercial basis, not to mention the technical assistance available free or on credit, when complete plant equipment is imported on a deferred payment basis. Substantial tax-free profits are transferred abroad by foreign owned corporations under the cover of payments for the know-how and the patents.

From what was said above, it follows clearly that in our opinion foreign direct investment should be excluded from the category of foreign aid. At a time when so many developing countries are asked to promulgate 'codes of investment' giving privileges and guarantees to foreign private investors, it might be useful to enumerate the minimum conditions, which from the recipient country's point of view should be respected in order to make the inflow of foreign private capital useful, if not part of aid.

(*a*) Foreign private investment should be licensed from the point of view of branch allocation, localisation and concentration of foreign capital in different sectors of the recipient country's economy.

(*b*) Foreign owned enterprises should be submitted to the same taxation as local enterprises and their books audited by the officials of the recipient country's government, especially with the view of ascertaining whether the declared export prices are not too low and the declared import prices for materials and equipment are not too high.

(*c*) All payments abroad, including royalties, transfers of profits and repatriation of capital, should be limited and controlled.

(*d*) Reinvested profits should be treated as domestic private capital (e.g. the transfer both of these profits at any future date and also of the profits derived from their reinvestment should be prevented).

In all fairness, we doubt whether much new direct foreign investment would be available under these regulations. It should, however, be emphasised that the inflow of foreign private capital to the developing countries does not reach substantial levels even in those cases where economic conditions offered by developing countries are quite attractive. This can be explained by two sets of reasons: on the one hand, prospective investors consider that the political risk involved is very high (possible nationalisation or introduction of regulations of the type described above); on the other, there is no scarcity of good investment opportunities in the developed countries.

AID THROUGH TRADE

In the first part of this paper we have come across several interconnections between trade and aid. In particular, the following points were stressed.

(*a*) Of the two functions of foreign aid—adding to the import capacity and increasing the financial resources of the recipient country—the former is the most important.

(*b*) In the long run, the capacity to service the foreign debt depends anyhow on the progress achieved by the recipient country in export promotion (and import substitution, it is true), so that an inflow of foreign aid does not as yet constitute a lasting solution, permitting a sustained and satisfactory rate of economic growth.

(*c*) A positive shift in the terms of trade is comparable to a continuous inflow of grants with no strings attached.

This leads us to the consideration of 'aid through trade', by which we mean either measures aimed at improving the conditions of existing trade (improvement in the terms of trade) or the creation of additional markets above the 'normal' volume of trade.[29] The opening of such additional export opportunities would increase the capacity of the developing countries to import and, thus, permit a higher rate of growth.

To the extent to which these additional exports would consist of sales of accumulated stocks, they would mean releasing reserves previously accumulated but 'frozen', as they could not be either traded or consumed. This would bring about either an increase in the personal disposable income without a corresponding decrease in the level of investment or an increase in investment with an unchanged level of consumption.

In the case of exports from idle capacities, the national income would increase over the level previously assumed without any additional investment. The aggregate capital–output ratio would be correspondingly reduced and either the country concerned could achieve a higher overall rate of growth with an unchanged relative share of investment in the national income or it could implement the assumed rate of growth with a higher relative share of consumption. These effects would be comparable to those arising from the provision of foreign aid, with two differences, however, namely that on the one hand, the aggregate expenditure would not exceed the national income, because no inflow of capital occurs, and on the other, the country would not become indebted.

Even the opening of markets for new lines of exports which do require investment but have a relatively favourable 'investment efficiency ratio' (cost of investment per unit of earned foreign currency) might be considered as 'aid', as it helps the assisted country to overcome the barrier of foreign trade with a smaller volume of investment, i.e. it improves its economic performance by lowering the aggregate capital–output ratio. This applies in particular to enabling the developing countries to export certain types of finished goods or semi-manufactures.

'Aid through trade' could include both multi-lateral and bi-lateral measures. While wishing all success to the search for worldwide schemes, evolved with a view to stabilising commodity prices and regulating international trade, we should like to offer below two suggestions to be explored in bi-lateral relations. Although they are less spectacular than these schemes, they offer some advantages: they can be easily put into practice, at least between countries having some measure of long-term planning; moreover, they seem to offer a good and realistic point of departure for the process of integrating the economies of developing countries, step-by-step, on a regional, or on a wider, basis. We have in mind long-term export contracts with stable prices, and the so-called branch industrial agreements.

Long-Term Export Contracts

These contracts should cover, first of all, the traditional exports of the developing countries, such as tropical foodstuffs, other cash crops, minerals, oil, metals and also semi-processed and finished goods, the production of which may be easily expanded. The contracts should provide for growing volumes of sales at stable or partly stabilised prices, by means of clauses either stipulating the maximum amplitude of the price fluctuation admissible in a year or establishing a procedure about the sharing between the buyer and the seller of the difference between the price agreed upon in the contract as 'basic' and the price actually quoted on the commodity exchange or considered by the two parties as representative of the 'world price'.

Quite obviously such contracts would give the planners in the developing countries a fair degree of certitude with respect both to future incomes from feasible exports and the volumes involved, so that they could take decisions about investment in advance. This knowledge of the trend of future trade is particularly important for perennial crops, when decisions about planting new trees precede the first crop by several years and at the same time set the level of production for quite a long period. Generally speaking, fluctuations of income from exports due to both price and volume variations have been affecting the economies of the developing countries so adversely[30] that even where a chance of future higher prices exists a premium on stability is worth paying.

Those partners of the developing countries who have a planned or even a directed economy should normally also be interested in knowing in advance what supply of specified goods they may obtain from given sources and what would be the cost involved. Stability is always welcome to the planner and worth paying for by the renunciation of uncertain gains from shifts of terms of trade, which he is not likely to take into account in the process of planning anyhow. At any rate, for a country normally employing most of its productive capacities, it should be much easier to assist the developing countries by accepting stable prices than by extending credits, which have to be offset by a lower volume of internal investment or consumption.

So many schemes of price stabilisation have failed to materialise, that the plea to introduce stable prices in bi-lateral exchanges may seem very daring. But the least we can say, is that, in contrast to international compensation schemes, our proposal can be easily tested and introduced progressively. We are, morover, convinced that the mere fact of signing a certain number of long-term contracts with stable prices would bring about an attenuation of price fluctuations in the commodity markets concerned, thus paving the way for more ambitious and general solutions.

Industrial Branch Agreements

The long-term contracts discussed above apply in the first instance to already existing exports. But in the process of economic growth the developing countries should obviously establish new lines of exports and this requires a thorough restructuring of the international division of labour prevailing at present. It was suggested at the United Nations Conference on Trade and Development (see Doc. E/conf.48/c.2/REC/2) that a practical measure with this end in view could take the form of 'industrial branch agreements' based on partial division of labour between the countries concerned. On the basis of bi-lateral consultations between representatives of a given branch of industry, a long-term agreement would be drawn up, establishing over a given period of time a changing pattern of mutual supplies, not necessarily balanced, including raw materials, intermediate goods, final products and equipment, with a final aim of implanting in the developing countries new industries, partly or wholly export oriented, and at the same time creating complementarity of economies based on specialisation and partial division of labour.

The resolution adopted by the second Committee of the United Nations Conference on Trade and Development, referred to above, specifically mentioned the developing countries and the countries with centrally planned economies and linked the whole matter with supplies of equipment by the socialist countries on a deferred payment basis, so that industrial branch agreements appear as a generalisation and a complement of the 'self-liquidating credits' discussed in the second part of this paper. But a parallel can be drawn between this specific measure, devised for the expansion of trade between the developing countries and the socialist ones, and the so-called 'complementarity agreements' which were foreseen by the Montevideo Treaty as a means to promote regional economic cooperation in Latin America, which have seldom been put to practice.[31] Mutual guaranteeing of stable and growing markets for new exports and the adjustment of long-term plans to these decisions seems to be the only viable way of approaching the problem of the diversification of the pattern of exports of developing countries both in the context of regional integration and of a modified division of labour in the world economy.

CONCLUSION

At the end of this effort to clarify some issues related to foreign economic aid, we should like to stress the following points.

(*a*) Foreign aid essentially means an improvement of external conditions of growth, even though it adds automatically to the financial resources of the recipient country whenever it involves grants or credits.

(*b*) The impact of foreign aid on the recipient country cannot be properly assessed out of the context of a development plan.

(*c*) To evaluate the effort of a donor country two different yardsticks must be used, depending on whether the country concerned has free capacity at its disposal or not.

(*d*) Long-term credits repayable in goods are the most attractive form of foreign aid from the point of view of the recipient countries.

(*e*) Another advisable form of aid can be achieved without imports of capital through multi-lateral schemes of trade promotion, bi-lateral long-term export contracts on the basis of fully or partly stable prices, as well as the so-called 'branch industrial agreements'. 'Aid through trade' is thus a complement —though not an alternative—to 'pure' aid.[32]

NOTES AND REFERENCES

1. To quote the so-called Jeanneney report 'L'aide est une notion ambigué et sa mesure chiffrée malaisée' (*La Politique de Coopération avec les Pays en Voie de Développement*, Paris, 1963, 51).
2. For a good analysis of problems and policies of developing countries arising from pivotal scarcities and the role of foreign aid in relieving structural bottlenecks, see *World Economic Survey 1964*, Part I, United Nations, New York, 1965.

3. The necessity of making a distinction between the inflow of foreign capital and that of 'aid' is today more or less accepted. See e.g. F. Benham, *Economic Aid to Underdeveloped Countries*, London, 1961 and P. Rosenstein-Rodan, 'International Aid for Underdeveloped Countries', *Review of Economics and Statistics*, May 1961, 107–38. For an all inclusive treatment of aid see *inter alia* H. J. P. Arnold, *Aid to Developing Countries, A Comparative Study*, London, 1962.

4. When foreign aid is granted by a country with free productive capacity, such aid does not necessarily lead to a reduction of the gap in the rates of growth between the donor and the recipient countries, because it contributes to the simultaneous increase of these rates in both countries. The concern of the developing countries with over-taking the developed countries is thus misplaced: we should aim at a situation where massive flows of aid from developed countries will help the developing countries to achieve higher rates of growth and thus to reach higher absolute levels of income *per capita*, while contri-buting at the same time to a higher rate of growth in the developed countries and retarding therefore, to mutual profit, the moment when the two groups of countries will find themselves at the same level of income *per capita*.

5. By 'net inflow' we mean the inflow of capital less its servicing.

6. The indebtedness of the developing countries is increasing at an alarming rate. Developing nations are paying their debts at the rate of five billion dollars a year, as against less than one billion a year ten years ago. Some countries have to devote 50 per cent of the value of their exports to the amortization of their foreign debt. The total foreign debt of the underdeveloped countries rose to ten billion dollars in 1955, and at the present rate it will be ninety billion by 1975 (*Comercio Exterior de Mexico*, May 1965, 11).

7. We may consider non-existing branches of industry as 'supply-determined' at the level of production equal to 0.

8. The less the cost in local currency of a unit of foreign currency earned, the more effective is an export.

9. Of course, after having exhausted all the possibilities of less capital-intensive export-oriented investments.

10. In his report on the Conference on Development Aid held in Dar-Es-Salaam in September 1964, D. A. Lury refers to the point raised there, that some of the aid given to African countries is in fact working against development. 'It was alleged that aid to some countries was being used to build up a small urbanised élite which was losing contact with its fellow-countrymen. It is difficult to assess the true benefits flowing from the development of aid but at the

least it seems clear that it would be wise for recipients to follow the rule given by Dr. Kiano, Kenya Minister for Commerce and Industry in his speech at the beginning of the Conference: "Look Gift Horses in the mouth", *East African Journal*, December 1964, 30.

11. This point, rather obvious to economists from countries with experience in comprehensive planning, is being increasingly accepted today even by authors who represent a school of thought which for a long time denied the need to plan. See, e.g. J. K. Galbraith, 'A Positive Approach to Economic Aid', *Foreign Affairs*, New York, April 1961. At the UN Conference on Trade and Development the developing countries were pressing to get foreign assistance on a long-term basis in the context of development plans, instead of piecemeal annual commitments.

12. In their 'Proposals for the Creation of the Latin American Common Market' (Supplement to *Comercio Exterior de Mexico*, XI (5), 1965, 3) the four wise men of Latin America—José Antonio Mayobre, Felipe Herrera, Carlos Sanz de Santamaria and Raul Prebisch—speaking of 'common denominators' existing today among the developing countries, state their foreign trade problem as follows:

'Markets for the traditional export of our primary commodities are shrinking and closing, without new ones being offered for our manufactures. The trend towards imbalance in foreign trade is placing a serious brake on the economic development of many of our countries. And deterioration of the terms of trade is materially reducing the positive contribution of international financial resources to our development.'

13. For a not too satisfactory attempt to define different aspects of the 'absorptive capacity' see P. N. Rosenstein-Rodan, 'International Aid for Underdeveloped Countries', *Review of Economics and Statistics*, May 1961, (2), 107–38, and the criticism formulated by D. A. Baldwin and G. Ranis in the May 1962 and November 1962 issues of the same journal.

14. Compare for this point D. Dosser, 'National Income and Domestic Income Multipliers and their Application to Foreign Aid Transfers', *Economica*, February 1963.

15. From the point of view of the balance of payments the impact of import substitution is, of course, identical to that of additional exports.

16. To some extent, it implies the choice of a strategy for development. Some writers would advice the underdeveloped countries to concentrate for a certain period of years on investments in 'human

resources' before starting industrial investments. Such a strategy is open to two criticisms. On the one hand, it retards unnecessarily the beginning of the actual process of development. On the other, all plans for manpower training must rely on long-run economic plans, and not *vice versa*, the more so since vocational training in industrial crafts could not succeed in the absence of industrial plants.

17.   In an essay on 'The Political Case for Economic Development Aid' (mimeographed), Professor Max. F. Millikan of M.I.T. (Cambridge, Mass.) recognised that 'foreign aid is not a goal of the USA nor even a separable element in our foreign policy but rather a handy multi-purpose instrument of that policy which we have been tempted to use in an increasingly wide variety of ways for an increasingly broad range of purposes'. Time and again the American press opens the debate on the same subject. The conflicting positions are aptly summarised in the following excerpt from an editorial published by *The New York Times* (Int. Edition) on 12 January 1965: 'Some critics, taking the simplest, balance-sheet approach, insist that the *quid* of US aid must be held back from any country that does not provide the *quo* of support for American policies. But such a policy would be self-defeating. To try to make docile puppets out of aid recipients would lead to bribery and blackmail, destroying all that the programme has already accomplished and ending in complete futility.' The political functions of American foreign aid are clearly stated by H. Fois in his recent study on *Foreign Aid and Foreign Policy* (New York, 1964). For a brutal assessment of the strategic importance of developing countries for NATO and the consequent call to subordinate foreign aid entirely to political and military criteria, see M. W. J. M. Brockmeijer, *Developing Countries and NATO*, Leyden, 1963.

18.   Senator Fulbright is one of the American advocates of multi-lateral rather than bi-lateral aid. In a long article written for *The New York Times Magazine* and reproduced in *The New York Times* (Int. Edition) on 27–28 March 1965, he makes it clear, however, that he seeks only a 'psychological difference', as he advocates channelling American foreign aid through international institutions which are controlled to a large extent by the USA. 'It should be understood', writes Senator Fulbright, 'that while the World Bank and the IDA are independent international agencies, the influence of the USA on their policies is considerable because decisions on loans are made by votes weighted according to contributions. As the largest single contributor, the USA has the greatest voting power. In channelling its development loans through the IDA, therefore, the USA would

be renouncing exclusive control, with its attendant disadvantages, while retaining great influence on the disposition of its contributions.'

In an article on the World Bank's relations with India a contributor to *The Economic Weekly*, Bombay, 4 April (1964, 630), stated:

'Dispensation of aid has invariably been accompanied by dispensation of advice; the latter has varied from mild suggestions to outright interference in the policy formulations of the recipient country. We were hitherto at the milder end of the advice scale. We are moving, one fears, rapidly to the other end.'

The distinction between public and private loans proves, moreover, deceptive to the extent to which some public lending agencies, such as the World Bank, insist on the so-called 'bankability' of projects to be financed, extending the market test to projects in the public sector without much concern for the social external economies. This attitude has been criticised at the Geneva Conference on Trade and Development by representatives of developing countries.

19. For a recent study of aid provided by the Socialist countries see G. M. Prochorov, *Dvie Mirevyie Sistemy i Oswobozdivsijesia Strany*, Moscow, 1965.

20. For an analysis of the impact of 'grain loans' see, in particular: Said El-Naggar, *Foreign Aid to United Arab Republic*, Institute of National Planning, Cairo, 1963; Ch. Beringer, *The Use of Agricultural Surplus Commodities for Economic Development in Pakistan*, Institute of Development, Karachi, 1964; K. N. Raj, *Indian Economic Growth— Performance and Prospects*, New Delhi, 1965.

21. The counterpart funds are calculated from the dollar cost of supplies by applying a fixed exchange rate. For this reason and also because of the possible variations of stocks of grain, the counterpart funds do not correspond exactly to the proceeds from actual sales of grain.

22. *New Africa (London)*, July 1965, 6, commented on the action taken by the American Congress to withhold supplies of American grain to the United Arab Republic (a decision subsequently reversed):

'To withhold bread from the starving has never been considered moral. It is in the light of such considerations that the action of the Congress in using the surplus for political blackmail comes as a shock even to those who have become hardened to the realities of aid with strings.'

23. For an apologetic view of foreign direct investment, though sceptical about its volume, see, *inter alia*, the important book of F. Benham on *Economic Aid to Underdeveloped Countries*, London, 1961.

For an open criticism of aid through public channels and an out-right plea to increase the flow of private direct investments, see E. G. Collado, 'Economic Development Through Private Enterprise,' *Foreign Affairs*, New York, July 1963. H. Feis (*Foreign Aid and Foreign Policy*, New York, 1964) insists on the traditional philosophy of American 'free enterprise' with respect to the division of roles between public and private investments. The former should concentrate on infra-structure, in order to pave the way for the latter.

A 1963 amendment to the foreign aid bill voted by the US Congress requires that 50 per cent of development loans be channelled into private business activities. This measure was criticised even by a top AID administrator (see F. M. Coffin, *Witness for Aid*, Boston, 1964, 123).

24. In his lectures on *Indian Economic Growth—Performance and Prospects*, New Delhi, 1965, Professor K. N. Raj of the Delhi School of Economics, on the basis of data from a sample study of the Reserve Bank of India on foreign collaboration in the chemical industry, estimates that the total foreign exchange outflow per annum in the case of the companies with private foreign collaboration covered by the sample works out to nearly 24 per cent of the capital invested by the foreign participants, 'which is higher than the servicing burden on even the most onerous of loan capital received so far' (p. 23).

Dr. Raj reaches the following conclusion about types of foreign aid suitable to India:

'If our interest is in minimising the burden on foreign exchange we should really be concentrating on loans which either carry with them a long period of repayment or an understanding that the lending country will take more exports from India and help the whole process of repayment by raising the export earnings of the country. In the case of foreign private investment there is often a bias against export of the products concerned since investment itself comes now mainly from international companies which have similar stakes in other countries.

'It is only in the case of loans from the Soviet Union that aid has been closely tied up with trade, and this has produced good results. Though the annual servicing burden on Soviet loans has been nearly 12 per cent the rapid expansion in exports to the Soviet bloc in the last few years has made it possible to meet this liability without much difficulty. In fact, Soviet aid is really in the nature of trade credits tied to more trade, and this is advantageous to both the lending and the receiving countries. The Soviet Union is able to offer an expanding market for Indian products because it has need for them and because it is in its own interests to accept these products in exchange for the machinery and capital goods it exports to India' (pp. 23–4).

25.   Compare the well-known essay by E. D. Domar on 'The Effect of Foreign Investment on the Balance of Payments' originally published in the *American Economic Review*, December 1950, and included in his *Essays in the Theory of Economic Growth*, New York, 1957.

26.   Looking at the matter from a different angle, given a constant yearly gross inflow of capital (C), a rate of profits transferred abroad (p), and a rate of profits reinvested (q), the net inflow of capital will become zero after a certain number of years (n), which can be calculated from the following formula:

$$n = \frac{\log \dfrac{p + q}{p}}{\log (1 + q)}$$

With the assumption of our first case, i.e. $p = 10$ per cent and $q = 5$ per cent, the positive effects of a constant yearly inflow of C units of foreign capital would be entirely offset by the outflow of profits in the ninth year, while in the second case ($p = 5$ per cent, $q = 10$ per cent), the same effect would take place in the 12th year.

27.   Several limitations of direct foreign investment are recognised in a study on 'Balance of Payments Problems in Developing Africa', published in the *Statistical and Economic Review of The United Africa Company Ltd.*, April 1964 (29).

The author reaches the following conclusion:

'For developing countries with their current balances already in deficit or tending that way, an unduly large outflow—more particularly in the form of servicing charges, which are of a recurrent nature—is a matter of understandable concern and one apt to prompt them to impose those very curbs on capital and dividend repatriation which can only act to discourage further capital inflows in the future. Yet a point must be reached sooner or later at which the rise in the debt servicing bill has to be halted' (pp. 44–5).

28.   For an assessment of developed countries' vital economic and strategic interest in the natural resources of the developing countries, see M. W. J. M. Broekmeijer, *Developing Countries and NATO*, Leyden, 1963.

29.   'Despite—indeed because of—the greater resistances that must be encountered by aid in the form of market, as against aid in its

other forms, the case for its provision appears to be inescapable if the developing countries, certainly of Africa, are to succeed in developing their economies beyond the constraints of current domestic capacity and ahead of slowly moving economic forces. And, what is more, short of a sufficient enlargement of their export markets, however this comes about, it will become increasingly difficult to continue to put other forms of aid to profitable use: to continue, that is to use them to *promote growth* instead of to subsidise resistances to it.' ('Balance of Payments Problems in Developing Africa', *Statistical and Economic Review of the United Africa Company Ltd.*, April 1964 (29), 54).

30. During the last 50 years, the 18 basic tropical products, accounting for 90 per cent of their total, registered average annual fluctuations of 14 per cent with respect to unit-prices, 19 per cent with respect to the volume and 23 per cent with respect to the income from exports. Moreover, taking into consideration the costs of marketing, a 10 per cent variation of the final price means a 20–25 per cent difference in the income of the producer. (*La Politique de Coopération avec les Pays en Voie de Développement*, Paris, 1963, 95.)

31. Compare the following assessment, made in the 'Proposals for the Creation of the Latin American Common Market', by José Antonio, Antonio Mayobre, Felipe Herrera, Carlos Sanz de Santamaria, Raul Prebisch:

'As is well-known, the import substitution process is entering a new stage. Easy substitutions are wholly, or nearly exhausted, in the more advanced Latin American countries and technically complex industries are beginning to be set up requiring large investments and a sizeable market. None of our countries, no matter how large or vigorous, could begin or continue this stage of industrialisation on its own in economically viable conditions.

'It is therefore necessary to plan the development of these industries on a regional scale. This planning refers principally to iron and steel, some non-ferrous metals, some groups of heavy chemical and petro-chemical industries, including the production of fertilisers, and the manufacture of motor vehicles, ships and heavy industrial equipment. This involves a limited number of industries which, in addition to being import substitution industries, cover fields of vital importance for strengthening the economic structure and accelerating the pace of our countries' development. It is precisely in such fields that economies of scale, the advantages of suitable siting, the utilisation of productive capacity and better operational efficiency will be most strikingly achieved. One of the paradoxical situations existing side-by-side with the Treaty of Montevideo has been that some of these industries have been established or expanded in various countries without regard to the objectives of an integration policy.

'It would be appropriate for the governments to decide now to conclude these sectoral agreements in such industries so that a start can be made, without delay, on the studies needed for carrying out the relevant negotiations.

'One result of the investment policy in all these industries might be the conclusion of a series of sectoral agreements within the next few years. Although these agreements are provided for in the Treaty of Montevideo, very few of them have so far been concluded, and those that exist do not relate to the industries that are of basic importance.' (Supplement to *Comercio Exterior de Mexico*, May 1965, 8–9.)

32. This last conclusion broadly coincides with the prevailing opinion among the delegates of the developing countries to the United Nations Conference on Trade and Development, who quite understandably insisted on having the best of both worlds: a substantial improvement in trade and an increase in the net inflow of capital.

7

Problems of
Financing Economic
Development in a
Mixed Economy*

✤

I

The argument presented in this paper is based to a considerable extent on a distinction between two types of consumer goods: necessities and non-essentials. By necessities are meant goods which constitute a major part of the consumption of broad masses of the population. On the other hand, non-essentials are consumed mainly by richer strata of the population. The chief items in necessities are staple foods.[1]

We make the following two assumptions on the financial aspects of economic development:

(*a*) There must be no inflationary price increases of necessities, in particular, of staple foods.

(*b*) No taxes should be levied on lower income groups or necessities, so that restraining of consumer demand must be effected through raising direct taxes on higher income groups, or indirect taxes on non-essentials.

It will be seen that these two assumptions are of considerable significance for the course of economic development because they make it dependent to a great extent on the rate of increase of the supply of necessities.

* First published in Eltis, *et al.* (eds.), *Induction, Growth and Trade: Essays in Honour of Sir Roy Harrod*, Oxford University Press, 1970, 91–104.

II

Let us now consider a development plan for a medium period of, say, five to ten years. Let us denote the average rate of growth of the national income by r. We shall try to show that the rate of increase of the supply of necessities required in order to warrant the growth of the national income at a rate r without infringing upon our two basic postulates is a definite increasing function of r.

Let us assume for the moment that aggregate personal consumption increases proportionately to the national income, i.e. at a rate r, and that there are no major changes in the distribution of personal incomes between various classes of the population, such as those caused by the increase in the prices of necessities or by changes in taxation. Then to the rate of growth of the national income (r) there corresponds a definite rate of increase of demand for necessities (c_n). If the rate of growth of national income, and thus, of total consumption (r) is equal to the rate of increase of population (q), so that *per capita* consumption remains unaltered, the rate of increase of demand for necessities is equal to q as well. Thus:

$$r = q = c_n.$$

If, however, the rate of growth (r) is higher than the rate of increase of population (q), then *per capita* consumption will increase at a rate $r - q$ (approximately) and the rate of increase of demand for necessities *per capita* will be $c_n - q$, which will in general be lower than $r - q$. If we denote the average income elasticity of demand for necessities by e we can say that:

$$c_n - q = e(r - q) \tag{1}$$

where e is, in general, less than one. From this we derive:

$$c_n = q + e(r - q). \tag{2}$$

The average income elasticity of demand for necessities (e) depends on such elasticities for various classes of the population and on income distribution between these classes.

We also should take into consideration that, strictly speaking, e changes within the period considered. Indeed, as *per capita* consumption increases the income elasticity of demand for necessities tends to decline. This effect is the more pronounced the higher the rate of growth (r), so that e should really be assumed a declining function of r. But, as r is in fact a rather low percentage and the period encompassed is not very long, the influence of r upon e is of no great importance and may be neglected.

Thus e in equation 2 may be considered a constant, so that c_n appears to be a linear function of r. This is shown diagrammatically in Figure 1. The straight line (BN) inclined at less than $45°$ $(e < 1)$ passes through the point B for which both the abscissa and the ordinate are equal to the rate of increase in population (q). This point stands for the situation where there is no increase in total *per capita* consumption and thus the demand for necessities increases at a rate q as well. If $r = OM$ is higher than q, then the same is true of $c_n = MN$; however, c_n is less than r, the point N being situated below the $45°$ line (OQ).

III

We assumed in the preceding paragraph that total consumption changes proportionately to the national income. This, however, was intended merely to simplify a stage in our argument. In fact, it may be necessary, as will be seen below, to restrain consumption in order to allow for a more rapid increase in investment than that of national income. In such a case, consumption will have to be restrained by taxation. According to our rules of the game this will consist of raising taxes on higher income groups and on non-essentials. The question arises here whether this will not upset the functional relations between c_n and r arrived at above.

It should be noted, however, that the taxation of higher income groups or non-essentials will hardly affect significantly the consumption of necessities by the well-to-do. Thus the relation between the rate of increase of demand for necessities corresponding to the rate of growth of national income will continue to be represented with a fair approximation by equation 2 or Figure 1. Hence, c_n can be considered the approximate value of the rate of increase of supply of necessities which

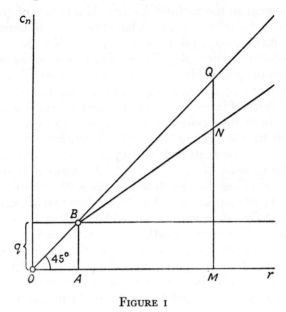

FIGURE I

warrants the rate of growth of national income at a rate of r without infringing our basic assumptions.

IV

The relation between the rate of growth of total consumption (c) and that of the national income (r) is of an entirely different character from that between c_n and r considered above. In order to sustain the growth of the national income at a rate r, a part of this income must, of course, be devoted to investment. Now the higher the rate of growth the higher the relative share of investment in the national income. Indeed, the higher the increment of the national income at its given level the higher the investment required in order to achieve it. Thus the higher the ratio of the increment of the national income to its level— or the higher the rate of growth—the higher the ratio of investment to the national income.

Imagine that we start from a position characterised by a rate of growth (r_0) to which there corresponds a certain relative share of investment in the national income. If this rate of growth is continued, the relative share of investment in the national income is maintained (unless, of course, there is a change in the capital–output ratio). But if the average rate of growth envisaged in the plan is higher so will be the average relative share of investment in the national income. This means that the relative share of investment in the national income will be increasing from the beginning to the end of the plan. (For instance, it may be 14 per cent at the beginning of a five year plan, 20 per cent at its end, and 17 per cent on the average.) The relative share of consumption in the national income will be correspondingly falling. In other words, the average rate of growth of consumption (c) will be lower than that of the national income (r). The difference ($r - c$) will be the higher the greater is the average rate of growth of the national income (r) in relation to r_0; because where r is higher the acceleration of the rate of growth as compared with the initial position will be greater and thus the increase in the relative share of investment in the national income will be greater in the period considered.

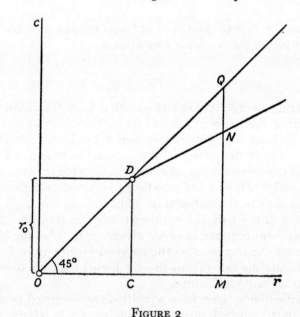

FIGURE 2

The relation between c and r is represented in Figure 2 by the curve DN. The point D represents the initial position at which the rate of growth equals $r_0 = OC$. If this is the rate adopted in the plan, consumption need not increase more slowly than the national income; i.e. $c = CD = r_0$. Thus the point D is situated on a $45°$ line (OQ).

If, however, the average rate of growth of the national income $(r = OM)$ envisaged in the plan is higher than r_0, the rate of growth of consumption $(c = MN)$ is lower than r and thus is below the $45°$ line (OQ), the difference $(r - c = NQ)$ being more marked the higher r is.

The rate of growth of consumption (c) as determined by the curve DN shows how much it is possible to increase consumption after a sufficient allowance has been made for investment required to sustain the growth of the national income at a rate r. If r is higher than the rate of growth in the initial position (r_0), the increase in consumption will have to be restrained by taxation to provide for the rise in the relative share of investment in the national income. (If this rise is effected through expansion of private investment the revenue from the additional taxation serves to create an 'offsetting' budget surplus.)

As already mentioned above, according to our basic postulates additional taxes will have to be levied on higher income groups or non-essentials. Thus the curve DN indicates what is the task of the government in checking the increase in consumption at a given rate of growth of national income (r) by means of this type of taxation.

V

Let us now consider the interrelation between the three rates (c_n, r, c). We shall consider the case where the capital–output ratio does not increase over the level at the initial position; however, all our subsequent argument also applies fully to the case where such an increase does take place.

Let us combine Figure 1 and Figure 2 in Figure 3 (the letters of Figure 2 are now put in brackets to avoid confusion). It will be noticed that $r_0 = [O][C]$ is greater than $q = OA$. Thus the rate of growth of national income in the initial position is assumed here to be higher than the rate of increase of population.

It is clear that of the three rates of growth in question (c_n, c, r) our diagram determines two if one is given. Now, in underdeveloped mixed economies, it is the rate of increase of supply of necessities (c_n) that can be considered as given. The increase in production of necessities, especially of staple food, is limited by institutional factors, such as feudal landownership and domination of peasants by merchants and money lenders. As a result, the average rate of increase in the supply of necessities over the planning period (c_n) is kept down to a rather low level. It is true that supply of necessities is not identical with their production because they can be procured through foreign trade. We shall consider this problem at a later stage; for the time being we shall abstract from it, so that c_n is directly affected by the institutional barriers to the development of agriculture.

From the ceiling of the average rate of increase of supply of necessities which we denote by $c_{n\ max}$ we can determine by means of our diagram the rate of growth of the national income (r) and that of total consumption (c). We draw a horizontal line at the level OE, find the point of intersection F with the straight line BN, project this point downwards and thus obtain $r = [O][G]$ and $c = [G][H]$.

In other words, the rate of increase of supply of necessities ($c_{n\ max}$), as fixed by institutional barriers to the development of agriculture, determines the rate of growth of national income (r) which is warranted without infringing our basic postulates. Next is determined the rate of growth of total consumption (c) which makes a sufficient allowance for investment required for the expansion of the national income at a rate r. In order to restrain the increase in total consumption to the rate c, appropriate taxation of higher income groups and non-essentials must be devised. This seems to me the gist of the problem of financing economic development in a mixed economy.

According to this conception the main 'financial' problem of development is that of adequate agricultural production. The key to 'financing' a more rapid growth is the removal of obstacles to the expansion of agriculture, such as feudal land-

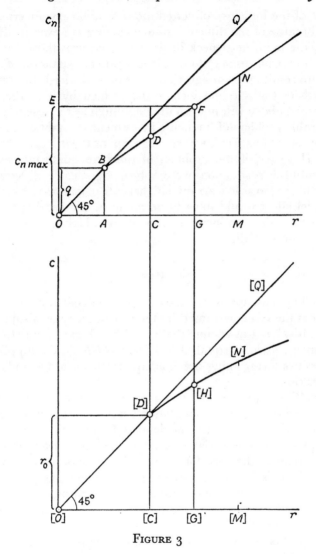

FIGURE 3

ownership and domination of peasants by money lenders and merchants.

The other strictly financial problem of levying taxes on higher income groups and non-essentials is also very grave because of the influence of vested interests upon the government and because of the difficulty of overcoming tax evasion. However, the main bottleneck in the balanced growth of a mixed economy seems usually to be the low rate of expansion of agriculture resulting from agrarian conditions. Indeed, the rate of growth of the national income determined by it in the way described above will not usually be so high as to present an insuperable problem of financing investment by taxation in such a way as not to affect low income groups or the prices of necessities. However, if the problem of the inadequate increase of agricultural production were solved by means of agrarian reform, etc., so as to warrant a higher rate of balanced growth, a parallel effort would have to be made in the fiscal sphere in order to achieve an increase in taxation of high-income groups and non-essentials.

VI

What happens, however, if the rate of growth of national income exceeds the level warranted by the rate of increase of supply of necessities? Let us assume that $r = OM$ is higher than OG (see Figure 3). Then, c_n equals MN instead of GF. As the supplies of necessities forthcoming are inadequate to meet demand their prices rise.

Equilibrium is restored through a fall in the real income of the broad masses of the population while the extra profits of the capitalists do not increase the demand for necessities, since they are spent on non-essentials or accumulated. Such extra accumulation reduces the need for taxation in order to finance investment. This is a reflection of the fact that the consumption of necessities, and thus total consumption, is restrained by the increase in their prices. It is true that this is partly offset by the extra consumption of non-essentials; but to the extent to which extra profits are accumulated, total consumption is on balance restrained.

Thus this type of growth involving inflationary price increases of necessities—against the first of our basic postulates—is definitely to the advantage of the upper classes. A relatively high rate of growth is secured without resorting to a radical reform of the agrarian conditions and with lower taxation of these classes than would be necessary if growth at this rate were balanced.

The aggregate consumption of the broad masses of the population is the same as it would be if the growth of national income were at a rate warranted by the actual rate of increase in the supply of necessities, i.e. it is the same at a rate of growth OM as at a rate of growth OG; employment is higher when $r = OM$, but real wages are correspondingly lower as a result of the increase in the prices of necessities. The higher relative share of investment which is necessary to increase the rate of growth from OG to OM is achieved at least in part at the expense of this fall in real wages.

Imagine that the planned rate of growth of the national income is OM. Allowing for the investment necessary to implement that plan, the planned rate of increase in consumption is $[M][N]$. This plan will be fulfilled but the rate of increase in supply of necessities will be GF and not MN and the rate of increase in the consumption of non-essentials will accordingly be higher. A corresponding shift will occur in the structure of investment: the development of industries producing luxury goods will be emphasized. The rate of growth will indeed be higher than OG, but growth itself will be lop-sided.

VII

We have so far disregarded foreign trade. However, for some countries this is a serious omission, because they are able to purchase necessities abroad in exchange for exports, especially in the case where they are endowed with rich natural resources (e.g., the oil-producing countries). We shall try now, therefore, to introduce foreign trade into our model.

The rate of increase of supply of necessities (c_n) stood for the rate of production of necessities when foreign trade was disregarded and it was on this assumption that the argument in section VI was based. If we introduce foreign trade, however, the straight line BN in Figure 3 ceases to represent the rate of increase of *production* of necessities (p_n). If imports of necessities can be increased more rapidly than their home production, the rate of increase of the latter is lower than that of the total supply of necessities.

Imagine that such is the case where $r = r_0$; i.e., where the rate of growth of the national income adopted in the plan is equal to the rate of growth in the initial position. Then, where $r = r_0 = OC$ the curve IP (see Figure 4) relating the rate of increase in *home production* of necessities (p_n) to the rate of growth of national income (r) which it can warrant without infringing our basic postulates, will be situated below the straight line BN (which shows the rate of increase in the supply of necessities which is needed at different growth rates). The gap between BN and IP is made good through foreign trade.

However, as r becomes higher than r_0, the difference ($c_n - p_n$) between the ordinates of the curves BN and IP will become smaller. Indeed, the higher the rate of growth (r) the more rapidly will the demand for imports other than necessities rise, and in particular the demand for investment goods. In general, it will be increasingly difficult to balance imports by a rise in exports because of certain limitations either of supplies of export goods or of foreign markets. Thus it will become increasingly difficult to increase imports of necessities at a rate which permits the increase in their domestic production to lag behind demand requirements. Finally, at the rate of growth corresponding to the point of intersection of the curves BN and IP home production and imports of necessities rise *pari passu*, c_n being equal to p_n. If the rate of growth of national income is pushed beyond that point, it appears that, in order to provide adequate imports of items other than necessities, the rate of growth of the domestic production of necessities would have to be higher than that of the required supply.

Figure 4 shows the influence of foreign trade upon the rate of balanced growth. Let us draw, as in Figure 3, a horizontal line at the level OE of the maximum rate of growth of production of necessities ($p_{n \, max}$). (We denoted this rate $c_{n \, max}$ in section V because $c_{n \, max} = p_{n \, max}$ if there is no foreign trade.) But now it will be the point of intersection of this line with the curve IP rather than with the curve BN that determines the rate of balanced growth. This rate of growth of the national income OK is higher than OG, which would prevail without the con-

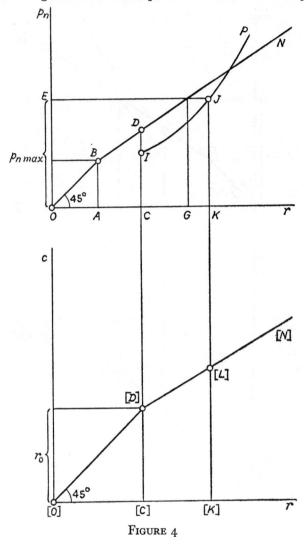

FIGURE 4

tribution of foreign trade to the acceleration of the increase in the supply of necessities. Such will be, for instance, the position in the oil-producing countries.

If, however, the foreign trade situation is less favourable, so that the difference $(c_n - p_n)$ at the lower ranges of r is smaller

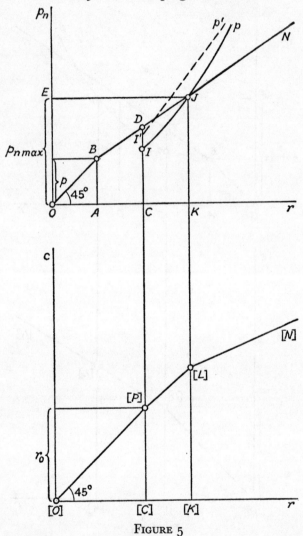

FIGURE 5

than in Figure 4, the contribution of foreign trade to the achievement of a higher rate of balanced growth may be nil (see Figure 5). The horizontal line at the level OE here passes through the point of intersection of the curve IP with the straight line BN.

Indeed, the position may even be reversed. Foreign trade may affect the rate of balanced growth adversely by aggravating rather than relieving the problem of the adequate increase of the supply of necessities. Such will be, for instance, the case if the relation between p_n and r is as represented by the dotted curve $I'P'$.

In the case where a favourable foreign trade position may permit a given rate of increase of production of necessities (p_n) to warrant a higher rate of balanced growth (r) the purely financial problem of adequate taxation of higher-income groups and non-essentials will, of course, grow in relative importance.

VIII

We assumed tacitly in the preceding section that imports are fully covered by exports, thus disregarding possible capital imports. We shall now consider the case where foreign credits are available to the government concerned for the period encompassed by the plan (which was not the case prior to that period). This eases the position of the economy with regard to the supply of necessities and thus makes possible a higher rate of non-inflationary growth. This is illustrated by Figure 6.

As a situation which would exist if no foreign credits were forthcoming, we choose the case where foreign trade does not contribute to the achievement of a higher rate of growth; the horizontal line at the level OE representing the rate of increase in the actual production of necessities; the straight line BN representing the rate of increase in the supply of necessities which warrants the rate of non-inflationary growth of the national income (r); and finally the curve IP representing the respective rate of increase of required home-produced necessities—all three intersecting at point J. As a result of the availability of foreign credits the rate of increase in the supply of home produced necessities which warrants the rate of non-inflationary growth (r) will be represented by the curve SZ situated below the curve IP. In consequence, the rate of non-inflationary growth will now be determined by the point of intersection T of the curve SZ and the horizontal drawn at the level OE. Since this point is to the right of J, the rate of non-inflationary

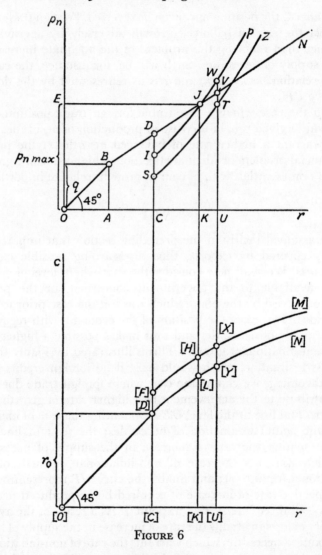

FIGURE 6

growth OU is higher than OK, which could have been realised in the absence of the import of capital.

It will be seen that, if there were no foreign credits, the rate of growth OU would require a rate of increase in the supply of necessities *UV* higher than *UT* and a still higher rate of increase in the *production* of necessities *UW* in order to cover the gap in foreign trade in other commodities. Foreign credits make it possible to reduce the rate of increase in the production of necessities for internal consumption to *UT* and to cover the gap in foreign trade in other commodities reflected in the discrepancy *WV*. Thus foreign credits will be used not only to supplement the home supplies of necessities but to make possible the required higher imports of other goods such as machinery or raw materials.

IX

Foreign credits affect, however, not only the problem of the supply of necessities and the balancing of foreign trade in other commodities, but also the problem of financing investment, and thus they reduce the need for taxation of non-essentials and higher income groups which is required in order to restrain the consumption of non-essentials.

Or, to put it more precisely: as a result of foreign credits the total supply of goods will increase more rapidly, in the period considered, than the national income. However, the relative share of investment in the national income, depending on the rate of growth of the latter, will not be affected. Thus at a given rate of growth of the national income, the time curve of investment will be the same as in the absence of foreign credits. It follows that total consumption will grow at a higher rate than it would have done at the same rate of growth of the national income if no foreign credits had been available. Since the rate of increase in the required supply of necessities (home produced or imported) corresponding to a given rate of growth remains the same, it is the consumption of non-essentials that will benefit and the need for restraining this will be accordingly reduced.

In the lower part of Figure 6 the higher permissible rate of increase in total consumption is now represented by the curve [*F*][*M*] which is situated above the curve [*D*][*N*]. To the rate of growth *OU* based on availability of foreign credits thus corresponds the rate of increase in total consumption [*U*][*X*] which is higher than [*U*][*Y*] that would correspond to *r* =

$[O][U]$ if no foreign credits were forthcoming. Since the required rate of increase in the supply of necessities corresponding to $r = [O][U]$ is UV with or without foreign credits, it is the rate of increase in the consumption of non-essentials that will benefit from $[U][X]$ being higher than $[U][Y]$.

X

It will be seen that, when the import of capital is used to raise the rate of non-inflationary growth by supplementing the home supplies of necessities, the reduction of the taxes required to finance investment appears merely as a by-product of the process involved. However, it is perfectly feasible that capital imports may be used solely for budgetary purposes. The rate of non-inflationary growth remains at the level OK while taxation of non-essentials and higher incomes is reduced. As a result the rate of increase of total consumption is $[K][H]$ and not $[K][L]$, the consumption of non-essentials rising correspondingly faster. If the increased demand is directed towards foreign non-essentials, it is reflected in their imports. In the case where home produced non-essentials are the object of this demand, the production of investment goods has to be kept down by the authorities if inflationary pressures on necessities are to be avoided and thus investment requirements have to be satisfied to this extent by imports. In either case, foreign credits are directly or indirectly wasted on non-essentials while economic growth is not accelerated, although in the second case, foreign credits seem to be used 'productively'.

It should be noticed that even in the case where foreign credits *are* used to raise the rate of growth of the national income it is by no means *necessary* to reduce the taxation of non-essentials and higher incomes which permits a relatively faster increase in the consumption of non-essentials in the period encompassed by the plan. Indeed, the relief in the financing of investment which is a by-product of capital imports may be used for an expansion of government expenditure for such purposes as low cost housing, health and education.

At this point the question may arise how it is that capital imports manage to benefit the country considered in two ways.

This, however, follows clearly from the two functions that capital imports perform: first, the availability of a certain amount of foreign exchange enables the country concerned to modify its *structure* of home supplies, e.g., to increase the supply of necessities; second, by raising the *volume* of home supplies without creating new incomes, foreign credits contribute to the economic surplus and thus they reduce *pro tanto* the need for domestic savings.

NOTE

1. It follows from this definition that the list of necessities will widen with the long run increase in the standard of living.

III   CASE STUDIES

8

Report on
the Main Current
Economic Problems
of Israel*

❋

The present report is the result of the inquiry which I carried out in Israel in August and September 1950 at the invitation of the Minister of Finance. In addition to the observations and recommendations contained in this report, I submitted to the Minister of Finance estimates of balance of payments in 1951 and 1952 made on the assumption that the recommendations would be implemented. These estimates, however, are too conjectural to be published.

In the course of my work I had numerous discussions from which I profited very much, and I take the opportunity to express my gratitude to the people who helped me in this way in my inquiry. In particular, I am indebted to Mrs. F. Dulberg, who assisted me considerably in preparation of this report by supplying statistical data and qualitative information, and by discussing with me the measures I suggested.

It should be finally added that the opinions expressed in this report are not necessarily those of the United Nations Secretariat of which I am an employee.

* Government Printing Press, Tel-Aviv, 1951, 23pp.

GENERAL OBSERVATIONS ON THE MAIN ECONOMIC
PROBLEMS OF ISRAEL

The main economic problems of Israel are at present:
   (*a*) Difficulties in equilibrating the balance of payments;
   (*b*) Inflationary pressures;
   (*c*) Some measure of unemployment.

All these problems derive to a great extent from the continuing large-scale immigration to Israel. The first two problems, however, would persist for some time, although on a smaller scale, even if immigration were discontinued now.

In the first half of 1950 the seasonally adjusted merchandise exports[1] amounted to only about 11 per cent of merchandise imports.[2] The import surplus of goods and services in this period was about one-third of the national income. A little more than half of the import surplus was covered by private gifts and transfers of capital in cash and kind, and public remittances, mainly from the United Jewish Appeal. A little less than half was covered by foreign loans, unblocking of sterling balances, etc. Thus the economy of Israel relied heavily upon capital imports, some of which were of the non-recurrent type, while the full recurrence of the other part was by no means assured. It is obvious that this creates an extremely precarious position for the normal functioning of the economy.

The inflationary pressures are mainly created by very high public and private expenditures on investment, by expenditures of the Jewish Agency and Keren Kayemeth for supporting new immigrants, and finally by the special military budget. The current administrative budget is balanced. The total net investment plus the support of new immigrants by the above bodies amounted, in the first half of 1950, to about one-third of the national income. However, the pressure exerted by this expenditure was roughly neutralised by a considerable import surplus. It is this neutralising influence of the import surplus that explains the fact of a relatively moderate inflationary pressure in the first half of 1950. The rationing of food in that period was not so much necessitated by the overall inflationary pressure as by scarcity of this item in relation to the aggregate consumption of goods and services. As to other goods, no acute shortages arose in the first half of 1950, although most of the prices were controlled on a level based on cost plus 'normal profit' calculation. The black markets were of limited importance. There was, however, probably some depletion of inventories of certain goods. In the main, inflationary pressure was concentrated in the free market for new apartments, which were sold by the building entrepreneurs at exorbitant prices.

But this state of rather moderate inflationary pressures was conditioned, as already stated, by the large import surplus. Any attempts at the reduction of the import surplus, while investment activity (inclusive of public works) continues unchanged, lead to increased inflationary pressures. This was clearly shown by recent events. The deterioration in the balance of payments position in the second half of 1950 necessitated a cut in imports which called for the reduction of some food rations and for the introduction of rationing of clothing. The result of these cuts in consumption caused a considerable intensification of the inflationary pressures, which manifested themselves in heavy buying of non-rationed goods and in increases in black market prices. This reaction, by the way, reflected not only the rise in current inflationary pressures but the anticipation of future shortages of commodities as well.

It is still necessary to consider at this stage the problem of the black market in foreign exchange which has some connexion with inflationary pressures and, at the same time, is of significance for the balance of payments problem. The accumulation of unspent liquid funds, combined with uncertainty about the future official rate of exchange, creates a natural tendency for illegal transfers abroad which depress the Israel pound in the black market in foreign exchange. Such a black market is the common experience of countries with a strained balance of payments necessitating the maintenance of exchange restrictions. In other countries, the 'unofficial' exchange quotations might have been disregarded altogether as having not much influence upon the economy. The case of Israel is different because of the importance of transfers from abroad. A considerable discrepancy between the black market and the official exchange rate of the Israel pound causes many of these transfers to be associated with the flight of capital from Israel instead of yielding foreign exchange. Foreign residents sending money to Israel or tourists credit certain amounts in foreign currency abroad to Israeli residents, who in return pay out an equivalent in Israel pounds according to the black market rate. Now, it is clear that any intensification of inflationary pressures will depress the Israel pound in the black market because a part of unspent incomes will tend to be invested in this way.

It should be noted that, in spite of the existing inflationary pressures, the Israel economy has been underemployed rather than overemployed. In the second quarter of 1950, unemployment outside camps amounted to about 10,000 (of which only a half was registered) or 2·5 per cent of the labour force. In addition, candidates for employment in the immigrants' camps numbered about 25,000, i.e. 6 per cent of the labour force. Apart from this, a number of people have been employed on public works of a not very urgent nature. This unemployment which exists despite the prevailing inflationary pressure of demand is accounted for mainly by shortages of foreign raw materials and of available capital equipment, as well as by the time-lag in adjustment of new immigrants. It should be stressed, however, with regard to the shortage of equipment that in some branches of industry considerable unused capacity exists. The position in such cases is roughly as follows. The home consumption of the goods manufactured in these not fully used establishments cannot be increased because this would involve higher imports, while exports of these goods have not yet been developed for various reasons. It should be finally added that, hand in hand with general unemployment, there is a scarcity of skilled labour of certain descriptions which may sometimes hamper the increase in employment for unskilled workers.

Before measures which would contribute to the solution of the problems described above are discussed, it is useful to consider briefly a theory which is often propounded in Israel. It is frequently maintained that all problems could be solved at one stroke by abolishing foreign exchange restrictions and domestic controls. It is suggested that direct investment of foreign capital would then assume such enormous proportions as to make possible not only the maintenance of present imports, but even their expansion and thus would create an age of plenty. This viewpoint is, I think, entirely unrealistic. Although no analogies can be fully convincing in such matters, it may be useful perhaps to consider briefly the example of Mexico which has not had any exchange restrictions in the post-war period. It appears that that country, which is very well known to US investors and which had a high level of capital investment and total effective demand in 1947 and 1948, was able to attract, in that period, gross direct capital investment from the USA at a rate which amounted to only about 1 per cent of the Mexican national income. Although it may be maintained that the position of Israel in this respect is entirely different, this example may be useful for a moderation of the extravagant views upon the possible role of direct foreign investment in the development of Israel.

The measures recommended below go in exactly the opposite direction. It is advocated that the greatest possible effort should be made to reduce imports and to increase exports and thus to rely as little as possible on the import of foreign capital, while maintaining the strictest possible exchange restrictions. These measures for improving the current balance of payments will require a much larger degree of government supervision and interference than has hitherto been the case. In addition, the results achieved in this sphere will, as stated above, aggravate the inflationary pressures at home and thus call for an even more vigorous anti-inflationary programme in terms of direct controls and taxation.

The discussion of measures advocated below for at least a partial solution of the main current economic problems of Israel is arranged in the following sequence:

(*a*) Measures for reducing imports and increasing exports;
(*b*) Other measures for equilibrating the balance of payments;
(*c*) Anti-inflationary measures.

MEASURES FOR REDUCING IMPORTS AND INCREASING EXPORTS

Before dealing with such measures it will be useful to enumerate certain facts pertinent to the problem.

(*a*) As mentioned above, there exists in some branches of industry in Israel significant excess capacity which could be used for production for export.

(*b*) In some cases, finished commodities are still imported which could be manufactured in Israel with the existing capital equipment.

(*c*) It is possible in some cases to save on imports by changing the method of production with the existing equipment so as to use more labour and home materials and less imported materials.

(*d*) In many branches of industry in Israel, only the relatively advanced stages of production exist while semi-manufactures are imported. Investment which would provide for production of semi-manufactures would, of course, make possible considerable savings in imports.

(*e*) Production of finished investment goods (machinery, etc.) is very little developed in Israel. Here also savings in imports could be achieved by developing the respective industries where suitable conditions exist.

(*f*) In certain instances, the new industries working under particularly favourable conditions may not only cover the needs of the home market but may develop exports.

(*g*) Israel is entirely dependent on imported fuel which is now the largest single item in imports. While the search for sources of fuel should be vigorously pursued some economies in the use of fuel could be achieved immediately.

(*h*) Israel imports large quantities of food and fodder. At the same time there are considerable reserves of land where agricultural production can be developed with a relatively small investment in irrigation. It is clear that such a development means a considerable saving in imports.

(*i*) As to the export of agricultural products, a considerable expansion of citrus fruit production will take a rather long time, but exports of vegetables and preserves may be increased in the near future.

(*j*) There exist possibilities for growing certain industrial raw materials which could be used either for export or for the home industry.

(*k*) Because of the poor natural resources of Israel, waste collection which can provide substitutes for imported raw materials is of special importance.

Export Drive

Considerable excess capacity exists in Israel—especially after the recent cuts in home consumption—in such light industries as textiles, apparel, shoes, leather goods, etc. This capacity could be mobilised for exports, provided markets were found for such products abroad. As for obtaining, where necessary, an import quota, Israel is in the favourable position of having an import surplus with practically all countries, which is covered to a considerable extent in dollars. This, of course, improves Israel's bargaining power with regard to the type of its exports to which these countries would agree in concluding commercial agreements. However, in all instances, whether the problem of import quotas does or does not come into consideration, Israeli goods of this type are too expensive and require considerable export premiums. It is essential that such premiums be granted, even if they should amount to a relatively high percentage of the value added.

Export premiums should nevertheless be kept as low as possible and other inducements should also be used for expanding exports. The allocation of raw materials for production for the home market should be made dependent on the export performance of firms so that they will be encouraged to export at prices lower than those achieved on the home market. It may be added that in bi-lateral trade export premiums are now frequently concealed in the form of higher prices for imports. It is clear that when adequate 'open' export premiums are granted, imports will have to be made at normal prices.

The desirability of exports should not obscure the danger inherent in the exchange of Israeli products, for which the cost of foreign raw materials accounts for a considerable proportion of the export price, against imports of other commodites. If such a transaction is not carefully watched, it may not result in any substantial gain and may even involve a loss. For instance, in the case of worsted woollen fabrics, the cost of imported yarn is more than 60 per cent above the export price. It may very well happen that such goods are exchanged against not very essential commodities or at a rather unfavourable price relation. In such a case the same, or an even better, effect may be achieved by foregoing production for exports and using exchange spent on worsted yarn for purchase of more essential goods at lower prices. Another instance is the export of automobiles assembled in Israel from parts imported from the USA. The above points to an additional reason for the desirability of building up the basic stages of production in Israel.

Immediate Savings in Imports
In spite of a severe shortage of foreign exchange some finished commodities are still imported which could be manufactured with existing capital equipment. An important instance is the importation by the Jewish Agency of tents which could be manufactured in Israel.

It is possible in some cases to change the pattern of production in such a way as to use more labour and home materials and less imported materials without any new capital investment. We shall limit ourselves here to one important example relating to building, which is the largest single industry in Israel. It appears that through certain changes in the system of building, which involve more labour and bricks or stone, considerable quantities of imported iron and cement may be saved. For instance, re-inforced concrete skeletons in three-storey houses may be replaced by self-supporting brick walls. Instead of re-inforced concrete ceilings ribbed hollow block ceilings may be built. Furthermore, most immigrant houses are now built on heavy soil and the floor consists of a re-inforced concrete plate suspended on piles. This system could be replaced by digging channels 1·80–2 m. deep and filling them with concrete made of cement and big stones.[3] The total cost in Israel pounds in all these instances, would be significantly higher than under the present system. As a large proportion of building in Israel is financed by the government, this raises the financial problem of increased governmental expenditure. It should be taken into consideration, however, that, if the additional labour required for building or brick making were transferred from less urgent public works, the expenditures on these could be correspondingly reduced. This offset to increased costs, of course, would not appear if new workers were hired. In such a case, however, a contribution to the elimination of unemployment would be made.

Investment for Reducing Imports or Expanding Exports

As mentioned above, in many industries in Israel only a relatively advanced stage of production exists, semi-manufactures being imported from abroad. For instance, in the cotton industry there exists only weaving and thick yarn spinning while thin yarn is imported at a cost three times as high as that of raw cotton. It is, therefore, clear that a considerable saving in imports may be achieved by investment in basic industries. In many instances, the cost of investment is small in relation to the saving in imports, the value added *per annum* being up to three to four times as much as the value of the machinery required.

Israeli industry frequently is not only lacking the lower stages of production but is also very poorly developed in the sphere of finished investment goods (machinery, etc.). The smallness of the internal market is an important obstacle to the development of production of some goods. Nevertheless, considerable possibilities of suitable expansion exist. For instance, where there is a sufficient demand for spare parts of definite types, it would be very advantageous to develop their production. The same is true of certain types of machinery and precision instruments.

Where the new industries work in Israel under favourable conditions of supply of raw materials and skilled workers they can, of course, be built up into export industries. In this connexion the resources of the Dead Sea are of great importance and their exploitation should be started as soon as possible. There is also an ample raw material basis for the cement and earthenware industry. Building up of a petro-chemical industry (production of organic chemicals from petrol) is favoured by the availability in Israel of many trained chemists. Good prospects also exist for development of the manufacture of some types of machinery and of precision instruments. However, the development of such industries as the production of precision instruments requires an immediate establishment of training schemes in the existing workshops which should be financially supported by the government. Similar arrangements should be made in other industries where development is hampered by a lack of highly skilled labour.

In the preceding two paragraphs the type of industrial investment which would reduce imports and increase exports was briefly outlined. It should now be stressed that all investment in industry should be largely concentrated on these two tasks. Indeed, a very large part of the machinery involved in industrial investment has to be imported, and in view of the strained position of the present balance of payments the foreign currency available for this purpose is limited. It is thus necessary to follow the principle that foreign currency can be spent on investment goods only provided that foreign currency is saved in the future. Investment in branches of industry where unused capacity still exists, even though the process would involve considerable modernisation, is a luxury that the Israeli economy cannot afford for the time being. This is especially the case because, as follows from the above considerations, there is no scarcity of labour at present, and therefore this sort of modernisation, which would aim at saving labour, does not make much sense from the point of view of the interest of the economy as a whole. It may be argued that modernisation is necessary in order to reduce costs and thus increase the ability to compete abroad, which would increase exports. Nevertheless, from the point of view of saving foreign currency, which is the scarcest factor in the Israeli economy, it is much more reasonable to pay export premiums, however unnatural such a subsidisation of obsolete methods of production might appear.

It follows directly that all investment in Israel should be very strictly supervised by public authorities. In order to provide these authorities with the possibility of greater differentiation between various projects, it might be useful to introduce a general import duty on machinery so that the authorities concerned would have the choice of prohibiting an investment altogether, approving it without any exemption from the duty on machinery, or exempting it fully or partially from that duty.

Organisational Problems Raised by the Above Suggestions
The above suggestions, involving in particular an immediate steep increase in industrial exports and a rigid control of invest-

ment from the point of view of its effectiveness in saving foreign exchange, cannot be achieved without supervision and prompting by public authorities. This should be done by the industrial controllers. They should investigate whether an investment intended by a firm is really advisable from the point of view of achieving savings in foreign exchange. On the other hand, if an investment they consider desirable is not forthcoming, they should create a government or mixed company which would build up the establishment required. The controllers should also coordinate the importation of machinery with the assurance of a steady supply of materials so as to avoid delays in utilisation of equipment. Such delays would mean a tying up of foreign exchange which would be unfruitful from the point of view of saving imports or increasing exports.

As to the expansion of exports, the controllers should exercise pressure on industrialists by refusing allocation of raw materials for the home market if no adequate exports are forthcoming, while keeping export premiums as low as possible. In order to be able to carry out this task, the controllers will have to secure a steady flow of imports of raw materials for the industry concerned. The controllers should check on the proper invoicing of export prices. Indeed, if the exporter invoices the export price too low, he is able both to retain abroad some of his export proceeds and at the same time to get a higher export premium. This problem also exists with regard to the import prices which may be invoiced too high because this provides another opportunity for capital flight abroad. The controller should be able to create, when necessary, a government agency in which would be vested all export and/or import activities of an industry. In so far as exports are concerned, the agency would buy from manufacturers at the lowest prices possible and sell abroad, covering the difference between these prices and the export price by premiums.

While the controllers would perform the above tasks with regard to their industries, they should be responsible for each task to the functional bodies which deal with the respective problems for the economy as a whole. Thus a body should be created which would control all industrial investment and would decide upon investment applications passed to them by the industrial controllers according to priorities based on the maximum savings in foreign exchange. Furthermore, a body should be created for the development of exports to which the industrial controllers would report on the progress of exports. This body would, at the same time, take part in the shaping of commercial agreements with the view of providing the industries with appropriate export markets, would look for other new markets, would enforce the export standards required, etc.

Savings on Imports of Fuel
Israel is entirely dependent on imported fuel which is now the largest single item in imports. It is still uncertain whether any supply from home sources may be achieved in the near future. The geological structure of the country points to the likelihood of the existence of oil deposits but they have not yet been found. The search for oil should be vigorously pursued. The practical possibility of obtaining cheap fuel oil and diesel oil from the existing deposits of bituminous limestone has not yet been fully investigated. Any scheme of exploitation of water power would involve very heavy capital expenditure and would not yield any tangible results in the next few years. Thus the only immediate way of reducing imports of oil is to economise in its use as much as possible. One of the many possible economies is the shifting of loads of bulky goods from road to rail transport, since the latter requires much less fuel per ton. Another is the reduction of transport of building materials by utilising to the greatest possible extent the building materials available close to a given locality (e.g., stone in hilly regions, bricks close to brick factories, etc.).

Reduction of Food and Fodder Imports and Increase in Agricultural Exports
As a large part of Israeli imports is accounted for by food and fodder, it is clear that the rapid expansion of agricultural production reduces considerably the volume of imports. The main factor in this process is the existence of large reserves of land on which agricultural production could be increased without a large-scale investment in irrigation. From the point of view of saving foreign currency, the pattern of the new agricultural

production is extremely important. It should provide for a maximum *net* saving in the volume of imports required to maintain the standard of nutrition. On the other hand, it will be necessary to put up in many instances with the higher cost of the home products replacing imports. In particular, where new cultures are introduced, this discrepancy may be considerable, but it should be tolerated with the proviso, of course, that in subsequent years it will be appropriately reduced.

The higher cost of home-produced food replacing imports will have to be offset by subsidies if the cost of living is to be maintained. This may appear 'unnatural'. However, it is really the present situation that is unnatural. Israel can buy its food cheaply abroad because, having a large import surplus, it does not, in fact, pay for it at all. The reduction of the import surplus will be achieved *inter alia* by producing food at home at a higher cost. Subsidies are merely designed to distribute the resulting disadvantages more equitably than would be done by price increases.

In order to save on imports of agricultural machinery, it is necessary to enforce the full utilisation of existing farm equipment. Thus additional areas for cultivation should be allocated to settlements in possession of surplus equipment. Full utilisation of equipment is frequently prevented by inadequate supply of spare parts. Care should be taken that such parts be manufactured at home (see page 127), or failing this that ample stocks of imported spare parts be maintained. All the tasks mentioned in this section require, of course, as in industry, a strong enforcement apparatus.

With regard to agricultural exports, quick progress in exports of citrus fruit cannot be expected because the expansion of citrus groves will take a considerable time. However, opportunities exist for developing in the near future the export of vegetables and preserves. This would require in some instances an expansion of refrigeration facilities, both in storage and transport, and in some instances export premiums as well.

With regard to the development of the production of industrial raw materials, favourable conditions seem to exist in Israel for the development of large-scale flax planting. The fibre obtained in the experiments seems to be of very good quality and the harvesting can be handled by normal combines. The extraction of fibre requires some machinery but this is of a rather simple type and does not involve any heavy investment. The by-products, i.e. oil seeds and shives, are also very valuable. The flax fibre could be easily exported or could be used after a process of cottonisation for replacing imports of cotton. Oil from the seeds and the shives would find an application at home which would also contribute to the saving in imports.

Collection of Waste
In connexion with the scarce natural supply of raw materials in Israel, collection of waste is of very great importance. Collection has been recently organised of non-ferrous metal scrap, waste paper, better class rags, hair from imported hides, discarded tyres and leather scraps. Through this, important substitutues for foreign raw materials are gained which in the near future may result in considerable savings of foreign exchange. With adequate personnel the collection could be expanded further still. Some bottlenecks prevent the development of the collection of other types of waste. For instance, to stimulate the collection of iron scrap for export, it would be necessary to make a small investment in machinery for lifting and pressing the scrap. Inferior rags could be utilised with the help of appropriate equipment for the manufacture of roofing felt. There exist in Israel large amounts of various types of wood waste which could be utilised for the production of boards, etc., if proper equipment were supplied. Old lubrication oil could be collected and regenerated which would permit a recovery to the extent of about 30 per cent.

A few words should be said about the general organisation of the waste collection. For the time being the collection is being done separately for the various items. It would be of great importance, from the point of view of cheapening the process of collection in terms of labour and fuel, while at the same time expanding its total volume, if all the collection of waste were vested in one public company which might use the services of the existing private firms for sorting, etc. of the items in which they are specialised.

Employment and Reduction of the Import Surplus
The measures indicated above for replacing imports by home production or for expansion of exports will tend to increase employment provided consumption and investment are not reduced. In the case when consumption is cut and the goods released are exported, the level of employment remains unchanged. On the other hand, if consumption was cut without an increase in exports, merely in order to save on imports of raw materials, there would be a fall in employment.

If the policies advocated above were vigorously pursued and their employment effect not neutralised by cuts in investment, the existing unemployment would probably vanish in the near future. Scarcity of skilled workers of a certain type may be an obstacle to a rise in employment. This should be overcome by intensive training for which, where necessary, foreign instructors would have to be used.

Other Measures for Equilibrating the Balance of Payments

Mobilisation of Capital Transfers in Kind
The so-called 'non-payment imports' amounted in the first half of the year 1950 to about 17 per cent of total imports. They consisted of gifts, transfers of capital by immigrants and non-immigrants and of personal effects of immigrants. The last item amounted to 2 per cent of total imports; other non-payment imports amounting to 15 per cent of total imports included some food and clothing parcels, but the bulk were transfers of capital in kind of various types which were largely substitutes for transfers of cash. The actual transfers of cash in the first half of 1950 were much smaller and were mainly from non-immigrants. The reason for such a preponderance of transfers in kind was the more advantageous rate of exchange that was achieved in this way. The sale of goods imported on the home market yielded more in terms of Israel pounds than the exchange of currency at the official rate. Even if the goods were offered for sale to public authorities, which in some instances

has been the case lately because of the prohibition of imports for free sale, some premium was offered and to this should be added the importer's profit. Finally, investment goods were imported for starting a business for which no licence might be obtained otherwise.

Initially, many non-essential goods were imported on a non-payment basis. However, at a later stage such imports were prohibited. This was done partly because some such imports were financed by illegal transfers of Israeli currency abroad. Thus recently, licences have been granted only for:

(*a*) Goods within the import programme to be sold to public authorities.

(*b*) Investment goods on the basis of affidavits confirming their *bona fide* character (i.e. that the machinery, etc. is intended for owner's use and not for resale and that they are financed from abroad and not by illegal transfers of Israeli currency).

Some of these licences, but not all, were processed through the Investment Centre. This system has deficiencies of two different types. On the one hand, the affidavits are not a sufficient guarantee that imports are *bona fide* and sufficient control is not exercised over the usefulness of the investment goods concerned from the point of view of the general investment plan. On the other hand, the premiums granted by public authorities for imports of essential goods seem not to have been sufficient to maintain a reasonably large influx of such imports. A line on which the scheme of non-payment imports could be profitably operated is indicated tentatively below.

The purpose of such a scheme is to convert the non-payment imports either into goods necessary from the point of view of the general import plan, or into cash transfers, while not reducing the total value of capital transfers. It is suggested that an immigrant should be given three alternatives.

(*a*) He could bring in his capital in cash at a substantial premium which, however, would be considerably below the discrepancy between the official and black market exchange rates of the Israel pound.

(*b*) He could bring with him some approved essential goods for sale to public authorities, also at a premium, which, however, should be less than the above premium on cash, because the immigrant will have the benefit of importer's profit.

(c) He could bring with him equipment for the establishment of business which must, however, be approved by the Investment Centre.

It should be emphasised that the alternative (a) of a cash premium is of great importance for poorer immigrants because (b) and (c) will involve, as a rule, relatively large transactions.

As to the non-immigrant capital transfers, they could be carried out in the way indicated in points (b) and (c), that is, they should take the form of imports of essential goods for sale to public authorities with a substantial premium, or of imports of equipment for establishment of enterprises approved by the Investment Centre. The Centre should also check whether the transaction is not likely to have been financed by illegal transfer of Israeli currency.

I hesitate to suggest a premium for non-immigrant cash transfers and this for the following reasons:

(a) The transfers of this type are not insignificant and one runs the risk that the existing transfers may be maintained at their value in Israel pounds so that the proceeds of foreign exchange on this account would fall.

(b) As long as the paying of premiums applies to immigrants only it can be interpreted as merely granting them certain favours. When applied to all cash transfers, it may be considered as a partial adjustment to the black market quotations which may be expected to go later on even further than the premium granted. This may both encourage illegal transfers abroad and may also cause some senders to temporize with their transfers.

(c) The illegal transactions at black market rates which are more profitable than sending cash at the premium described above are probably more developed for non-immigrant than for immigrant transfers.

The volume of useful non-payment imports and cash remittances from abroad will, of course, greatly depend on the rate of exchange of the Israel pound in the black market. The higher the rates, the more favourable will be the prospects for obtaining more in terms of legal cash remittances and useful non-payment imports. Indeed, in such cases, remittances combined with the illegal transfers of Israeli funds abroad will become less attractive as compared with legal channels. It seems, therefore, of great importance to improve the black market rate of exchange of the Israeli pound. The only way to achieve it is through such an absorption of the existing liquid funds in Israel as would make scarce the money available for illegal transfers. This problem will be discussed in some detail in the section dealing with anti-inflationary measures.

Foreign Exchange Profits from Parcels
The above suggestions do not cover food and clothing parcels, although these are also frequently in lieu of cash transfers and may even be financed by small illegal transfers of Israeli funds abroad. It is impossible to restrict the sending of such parcels because in present conditions it could cause widespread dissatisfaction among the Israeli population and their relatives abroad. They should, therefore, be permitted to continue with appropriate limitations per family and subject to customs duties. The government, however, could, so to say, go into the parcel business itself and in this way make substantial profits in foreign exchange. This is particularly important now that the aggregate volume of parcels is likely to increase steeply as a result of the reduction of food rations and of the recent introduction of rationing of clothing and footwear.

For this purpose the government should open agencies abroad, where the senders could pay in foreign currency for parcels delivered in Israel. These agencies should offer the delivery of standard food parcels of various types, as well as textiles, clothing and footwear, on the basis of samples. Special shops should be opened in Israel where the goods in question would be available against vouchers acquired by senders against foreign currency in parcel agencies. The prices of the goods in question to the sender should be competitive in relation to the retail prices in the country concerned plus freight. In the case of food, the government would make a profit to the extent of the margin between wholesale and retail prices. In the case of textiles, clothing and footwear, the government would gain the foreign exchange equivalent of manufacturing costs as well. Two factors would benefit the competition with normal parcels:

(a) quicker delivery, and (b) customs duty would be paid by the recipient only to the extent to which the commodities concerned would be imported.

Foreign Exchange from Tourists

The present arrangements for obtaining a certain minimum of foreign exchange from tourists by exerting on them pressure to exchange their foreign currency, so as to cover expenditure in Israel in advance at a minimum rate of $7.00 per day, are very reasonable. It is generally known that the expenditure of tourists in Israel is frequently financed by illegal deals consisting of crediting a certain amount abroad to an Israeli citizen and receiving from him the black market equivalent of this amount in Israel. Under the circumstances, securing firmly at least a part of tourists' expenditure in foreign currency at the official rate of exchange is a significant gain. An alternative arrangement might be to request tourists to buy certificates abroad which would be cashed in Israel. In such a case, they should also be caclulated at $7.00 or more per day for the expected stay and should not fall below a certain minimum of, say, $100 or $150.

It is clear that the improvement of the black market rate of exchange of the Israel pound would increase considerably the foreign currency revenue from tourists. As has already been said, this should be achieved by internal anti-inflationary measures.

Foreign Direct Investment and Foreign Loans

There exists in Israel a tendency to exaggerate the possibilities of foreign direct investment. Even if the encouragement of foreign investment provided by the Investment Law were successful in attracting foreign capital, it is doubtful whether this would provide a large volume of foreign capital in the form in which it is most urgently needed. The character of some major foreign investments which have been made so far may serve as illustration.

Some of these investments have as an object manufacture of goods for the production of which considerable idle capacity is available in the old established factories. The exports promised from the new establishments could be carried out by these old factories. In this event, they would perhaps require some export premiums, but no transfer of profits in foreign exchange would be involved which, according to the Investment Law, is permitted at the rate of 10 per cent of the foreign capital invested.

In other cases, enterprises are being founded for the export of goods for which the value added is low in relation to the value of imported materials. Now, if it is not very carefully determined whether or not the goods obtained in exchange for these exports are approximately as useful as, and are purchased at prices comparable to, those that might be obtained with the currency spent on purchase of materials, the transactions may not yield any substantial profit in terms of foreign exchange and may even result in a loss (see pages 125–6). It is true that if such a factory already existed in Israel, exports under strict control should be attempted. It is, however, doubtful whether this is the right type of foreign investment to be attracted by privileges granted under the Investment Law. It should be added that in some instances the foreign firm supplies only a part of foreign currency required for starting the enterprise and the Israeli government undertakes to provide the remainder.

As may be seen from the above, the direct foreign investment may frequently provide foreign capital of the type which is not particularly desirable. It seems, therefore, advisable to try out the possibilities of launching bond issues abroad in order to secure foreign capital which could be freely disposed of. The loans may be issued by the Israeli government or government-controlled development companies and should be financially attractive. For instance, the loan may be repayable gradually in the course of ten years, with a reasonable interest, and have certain features especially attractive to persons connected in this, or other ways, with Israel:

(*a*) The non-amortized part of the loan would be fully repayable on call in Israel at the official rate of exchange.

(*b*) Any amount of interest and amortization could be converted into Israel pounds at a substantial premium over the official rate of exchange.

It is, of course, impossible to say whether significant amounts of capital per year would be obtainable on these terms. However, such possibilities should not be left unexplored.

Mobilisation of Gold and Foreign Securities Held in Israel
A sizeable amount of gold sovereigns and foreign securities is held in Israel, and in view of the strained position of the Israeli balance of payments, the mobilisation of these assets is essential. The mobilisation of gold may perhaps be attempted in the following way. The holding and sale of gold in Israel would be delegalised. At the same time, however, holders would be offered an opportunity to exchange their gold against dollar or Swiss franc bonds issued by the government on reasonable terms of amortization and interest. The rate of exchange for sovereigns would be according to the current quotation of sovereigns in Switzerland. The amortization and interest would be paid in actual dollars or Swiss francs which could be used for importation of goods without licence. It is, of course, difficult to say in advance how much gold could be collected in this fashion.

The foreign securities held in Israel happen to be largely registered and therefore their surrender can be enforced. It is probably for this reason that the agio of their quotations in Israel over corresponding quotations abroad calculated at the official rate of exchange is much lower than that of the black market dollar. It will be, it seems, a fair remuneration to their holders if they are offered, in exchange for securities surrendered to the government, bonds offering such terms that their market value would be equal to the present market value of the foreign securities concerned in Israel. This would really amount to compulsory buying-off of foreign securities at their present market value, paying, however, not in cash, but in government securities of equal market value.

Remarks on the Problem of Devaluation
Such measures advocated above as export premiums, premiums on unpaid imports of essential goods sold to public authorities, premiums on foreign currency surrendered by immigrants, and finally, premiums on amortization and interest on foreign loans when converted into Israel pounds, amount to a partial

devaluation. It may, therefore, be reasonably asked whether the same results would not be achieved more simply by a general devaluation of the Israel pound.

It should first be stated that, while after a substantial devaluation export premiums could be abolished, even greater amounts in subsidies on imported consumption goods would have to be paid to keep the cost of living unchanged. It should be noticed that any significant increase in the cost of living which took place would otherwise immediately cause a rise in wages which would in turn contribute to a further rise in prices.

It should be further observed that devaluation would by no means encourage direct foreign investment. Indeed, export profits would not be in general higher, as compared with the situation where export premiums are granted. Home profits would also remain unchanged if the price–wage structure were not altered. At the same time the value of imported machinery in Israel pounds would be higher so that the rate of profit would fall rather than increase. If the mere problem of transfer of profits is considered, the 10 per cent of foreign capital invested guaranteed by the Investment Law would of course remain unchanged.

There still remains the problem of the influence of devaluation upon transfers of capital from abroad. As already said above, the premiums for foreign currency brought by immigrants, as also the premiums for non-payment imports of essential goods sold to public authorities, amount in fact to a partial devaluation. The reason why the premiums for cash transfers should not be extended to non-immigrant transfers have been given above (see page 135). Should it, however, be considered advisable to extend the cash premium to all transfers of cash, this need not be considered a reason for a general devaluation.

ANTI-INFLATIONARY MEASURES

It has already been stated that putting into effect the measures aiming at economising on imports or at expanding exports will aggravate the inflationary pressures. Indeed, any reduction in imports or increase in exports will have as a counterpart either an increase in incomes or a reduction in consumption if capital investment remains unchanged. However, since imports will frequently be replaced by more expensive domestic production and the value of new exports where premiums are paid will be lower than the incomes generated, the inflationary pressure will increase more than the import surplus will diminish. This will be reflected in the rise of budgetary expenditure on subsidies and export premiums.

It should be noticed that in so far as the replacement of imports by home production and the expansion of exports will involve transfer of labour from less urgent public works to agriculture and industry, government expenditure will be reduced and the inflationary pressure accordingly neutralised. It should be remembered, however, that unemployment in Israel also presents a rather serious problem. Thus the reduction of the expenditure on public works comes into consideration only to the extent to which the new demand for labour will be over and above the existing unemployment.

The measures advocated above for encouraging useful non-payment imports or surrender of foreign currency by immigrants will also increase the inflationary pressure, because as a result of additional premiums higher payments will be made to the recipients. Here, however, the inflationary pressure generated may be smaller than in the case of a reduction in the import surplus, because for the recipients these gains will be a 'one at a time' affair and therefore they will frequently not be spent on consumption immediately.

The basic anti-inflationary measure in Israel is a relatively well developed system of rationing and price control which safeguards the stability of the prices of essential goods. The rationing of food was working fairly well in the first half of 1950. Black markets were of limited importance then, but they have expanded recently. Although they are supplied partly by the sale of rationed food by some ration recipients, there is no doubt that a number of farms sell a part of their produce outside controls as well. In this way, the quantity of food distributed through the rationing system is diminished; or imports have to be increased in order to maintain the rations, which is an additional drain on foreign exchange. Thus the situation definitely calls for tightening up of controls.

Serious mistakes have been made in the introduction of rationing of clothing and footwear because it should have been preceded by a control of retail stocks. This would have made it impossible to hide or to sell in the black market the goods which were thus lost to the rationing system. The present scarcity of utility goods probably results from the fact that shopkeepers sold them illegally while keeping in stock for controlled sales more expensive goods on which the profit margins are higher. This discriminates against the poorer population and should be rectified as soon as possible by enforcing a proper supply of utility goods and their distribution by shopkeepers.

The market for new houses and apartments is for the time being not controlled. It is true that a large proportion of new apartments is allocated to immigrants. However, a significant part of residential building is still operated for the free market. In this way, the allocation of such a scarce commodity as dwelling space is being distributed not according to the urgency of needs but to the paying power of the buyers. At the same time, very high incomes are earned in 'free' residential building, and this, of course, contributes to the general inflationary pressure. It is therefore imperative that the occupation of all new residential buildings be controlled by the government or local authorities. All new dwellings should be allocated at controlled prices to immigrants and to hardship cases among the old population. It is quite possible that many of the entrepreneurs will stop building. They can easily be replaced, however, in building activity by the government or local authorities. It should be observed that not only has the boom in free residential building been permitted to develop without control, but, in addition, the distribution of licences has not been coordinated with the available supply of building materials. As a result, considerable black markets for these materials have developed. Even though such black markets have much less chance under general control of residential building, the coordination of the issue of building licences with the supply of building materials remains essential.

The direct controls, if effective, permit an equitable distribution of scarce essentials and prevent profits from accruing to producers of and traders in these goods. However, inflationary pressures cause the emergence of black markets, disrupt the price control of unrationed goods and finally affect unfavourably the 'unofficial' foreign exchange rate. It is, therefore, of paramount importance to collect the excess purchasing power by taxation. This can be done in various ways. One is a steep increase in the purchase taxes on non-essentials. Such an increase in indirect taxes, however, poses the problem of the rise in the cost of living and corresponding adjustments in wage rates. It does not seem probable that such adjustment would be very important. According to the information available, the average wage in Israel does not seem to exceed I£50 per month net of taxes and dues. It is not likely, therefore, that workers on the average spend much on non-essentials which would be subject to the additional indirect taxation. These taxes would really strike at the middle-class and the higher strata of the working class. However, the extent to which they do affect the budget of an average worker should be duly reflected in the cost of living index.

It is obvious that collecting the increased taxes on non-essentials is not only a matter of decree. High indirect taxes obviously tend to cause illegal sales. To prevent evasion it is best to collect the taxes as customs duties in the case of imported goods or from producers in the case of home produced commodities. Where, however, producers are small and numerous, this is by no means an easy matter. The efficient collection of the tax obviously requires an adequate number of competent and well-paid officials.

Another possibility is taxes on possession or renting of durable goods. One instance is the tax on private cars known in other countries. Moreover, rates on apartments rented or owned could be modified as follows. While they would be left unchanged up to a certain 'normal' level of the number of rooms per inhabitant, they would increase progressively with this number as it exceeds the norm.

The rates of income tax are fairly high and progressive in Israel but full collection is obtained only from wage and salary earners where the tax is collected at the source. It is generally known that only a part of the income tax due from profits, etc., is actually collected. Thus, in this area, the main effort should be concentrated on improving the estimates of taxable income and on collecting the tax due. This will require an increase in the number of competent officials, the treating at a disadvantage of those taxpayers who have no orderly accounts so as to induce the keeping of proper accounts, a cross-checking between the accounts of taxpayers, and finally the obtaining of information on their standard of living. It is essential to raise the salaries of income tax officials by means of special bonuses so as to increase their efficiency and to reduce the chance of corruption.

In addition to these measures of taxation, attractive opportunities should be created for current small and medium savings which would tend to relieve the inflationary pressure upon the scarce supply of goods. Two facts should be taken into consideration here.

(*a*) There now exists in Israel a widespread lack of confidence in the value of money.

(*b*) Most of the current saving is being done for the sake of acquisition of an apartment in the future.

It is for these reasons that an appropriate channel for small and medium savings may be provided by 'building certificates', the value of which would be guaranteed in terms of building costs. It is advisable to endow the certificates with a right of winning apartments by lottery. A certain number of apartments per year would be allocated for this purpose from the new residential buildings, the utilisation of which, according to the above suggestion, would be under government control. The certificates would be cashable at any moment at the value corresponding to the building cost index. The terms of building certificates are so favourable that their acquisitions should be limited to, say I£500 per year per person and they should be non-transferable.

The operation of the scheme can be managed as follows. The government would issue the certificates which could be bought from banks and post offices. The government would also publish each month an index of building costs, and if a certificate were cashed the value would be adjusted if building costs had increased from the date of the acquisition of the certificate. To introduce a certain brake upon the cashing of certificates, the upper limit should apply to the gross rather than to the net acquisition of certificates per year. (If, for instance, the upper limit being I£500 per year, a person buys I£300 worth of certificates at the beginning of the year and subsequently sells certificates for I£100, he is entitled to buy up to the end of the year only another I£200 worth of certificates and not I£300.)

The above measures aim at relieving inflationary pressures by current taxation and by creating attractive channels for small and medium savers. Another anti-inflationary measure can be conceived of as a 'one at a time' reduction of liquid assets (such as cash, deposits and securities). It is clear that the smaller the stock of such assets, the weaker, *ceteris paribus*, the tendency to spend on consumption or invest in black foreign exchange markets. The most appropriate form for such an operation is, I think, a compulsory loan for, say, I£50 million. The loan should offer reasonable terms of amortization and interest but should be absolutely non-transferable and not usable as collateral. Thus the loan, while gradually repayable with interest, should at present absorb the existing liquid funds without creating new ones. The compulsory loan should apply to all persons or companies earning profits over a certain level. It should not be fixed on the basis of income tax returns which are frequently fictitious, or on the basis of the value of bank deposits which may be irrelevant for the purpose, but on all sorts of varied information, quantitative and qualitative, such as actual likely income in the last few years, liquid and illiquid wealth, inclusive of probable foreign holdings, etc. To use one example, there is no doubt that the dealers in textiles, clothing and footwear made heavy gains during the introduction of the point scheme, and the building entrepreneurs have amassed considerable profits as well. Each of the persons or firms affected would have to sign a promissory note to pay the amount imposed in the period of a year or two and this would entitle the government to sue for default in the case of failure to meet the commitment. The banks should not make it easy to finance the payments by credits but on the contrary should exercise a restrictive policy. The payments should be permitted to be made not only in cash but in marketable securities as well.

While this operation would definitely relieve the pressure on the scarce supply of goods at home, it would probably be of

9

Financial Problems
of the Third Plan:
Some Observations*

❊

I

It will be assumed in what follows that:

(*a*) The development of the economy must not cause any inflationary increase in the prices of necessities;

(*b*) No additional taxes will be levied on necessities or on low incomes.

In view of the very low standards of living of the broad masses of the Indian population, these seem to me the basic postulates of balanced growth.

On these assumptions, to any rate of growth of the national income there should correspond a definite rate of increase in the supply of necessities, in particular of food grains. Indeed, this is true if existing tax rates are not changed (barring the case of significant redistribution of income before tax). But the necessary rate of increase in the supply of necessities will not be affected by additional taxes on higher income groups and non-essential commodities, since such taxation would hardly influence significantly the demand for necessities.

* Having gone to India for a three-month period (December 1959–March 1960) at the invitation of Professor P. C. Mahalanobis, Secretary of the Indian Statistical Institute, Kalecki did some research on the subject of the third five year plan, in particular on the problem of avoiding major inflationary pressures in the course of its execution. This hinged not only on correct financial policies *sensu stricto* but also on an adequate expansion of agriculture. First published in the *Economic Weekly*, Bombay, no. 28, 9 July 1960, pp. 1119–23.

Thus a sound financial policy must be based on two very different elements.

(*a*) A correct proportion between the rate of growth of the national income and that of the supply of necessities.

(*b*) A policy of taxation which would restrain the consumption of non-essentials to the extent that would provide sufficient resources for the financing of investment.

II

Let us consider first the problem of the adequate supply of necessities. It can be estimated that a 5 per cent increase in the national income *per annum* requires a rise in agricultural production at an annual rate of about 4 per cent. (The rate of increase in the production of food grains on the assumption that no imports would take place in 1965–6 would have to be even higher, namely, about 4·5 per cent *per annum*.)

Such an expansion of agriculture is a tremendous task which, I think, requires far reaching changes in the social and economic conditions prevailing in agriculture. I think that in the present outline of the plan, adequate provisions have been made for irrigation and fertilisers. On the other hand, I do not believe that with the agrarian conditions prevailing in India now, these facilities will be used to the full to produce the output required.

Agricultural holdings may be roughly subdivided into three classes.

(*a*) Relatively large or medium holdings, cultivated by peasants who own the land or have security of tenure with, or without assistance, of hired labourers.

(*b*) Small holdings cultivated by peasants who own the land or have security of tenure.

(*c*) Relatively large holdings leased by the owner to a number of small tenants without security of tenure either openly (in some States) or by circumventing the existing laws providing for security, through shifting the tenants around at short intervals, leasing land *de facto* to 'servants' or 'share croppers', etc.

The second category, i.e. small cultivators, though they do not suffer from insecurity of tenure, do not enjoy the conditions necessary for undertaking improvements such as availing themselves of irrigation facilities or engaging in minor irrigation projects, utilising more manure and fertilisers, improved seeds, etc. They are oppressed not merely by their inherent poverty but also by their dependence on the trader and money lender (who is frequently the same person). Being involved in a daily struggle for survival, they are not able to plan for the future.

The third category, i.e. owners leasing their land (frequently classified as having land under 'personal cultivation'), is by no means more promising from the point of view of expanding production than the second. The owners will be frequently of the rentier–landlord type, not particularly inclined to introduce improvements. The *de facto* tenants have no security of tenure and in addition they suffer, of course, from all the disabilities characteristic of small cultivators.

We shall try here to outline briefly a set of measures which would help to overcome to some extent the deficiencies of the agrarian structure that hamper the development of Indian agriculture.

With regard to increasing the viability of small holdings, it is clear that poor peasants are unable to carry out investment or even buy fertilisers and implements without the credit assistance of the government. It is also of great importance that they should be exempted from irrigation charges which frequently constitute an obstacle to the utilisation of existing irrigation facilities. However, no significant results from application of such measures can be expected unless the problem of the hold that the trader and money lender has on the small peasant is radically tackled. The peasant sells a substantial part of his crop immediately after the harvest at a low price to discharge, *inter alia*, his obligations to the money lender and at a later period buys grain for consumption or seed at high prices, and gets into debt again. A government corporation should buy and sell agricultural produce at fixed prices throughout the year thereby eliminating seasonal fluctuations. (Traders must *not* be used as agents for this operation because, in such a case, not much would be actually changed in the present set-up.) The government should also grant through appropriate channels short or medium term credits to replace the activities of the money lender. It is only in this way that the small peasant will achieve the degree of economic security necessary for undertaking basic improvements on his holding. The enforcement of ceilings for rents is also important in this connexion.

Let us turn to the problem of relatively large holdings which are *de facto* leased to tenants without security of tenure. A solution of this problem may, I think, be a properly scaled progressive land tax. The tax would have to be so high per marginal acre of relatively large holdings as to force the owner either to cultivate the land economically by introducing the necessary improvements, or to sell a part of it. In the latter event, a mortgage bank would have the option to buy the land. It would, in turn, sell this land to the actual cultivator (tenant without security of tenure, 'servant', 'share cropper', etc.) on instalment credit, the respective annual payments not exceeding the rent paid by him presently. (A more straightforward solution of the problem would, of course, be to grant security of tenure to all *de facto* tenants. Such a reform would, however, encounter considerable practical difficulties, given the present set-up in the countryside.)

It should be emphasised that the implementation of the measures outlined above offers a splendid opportunity for starting a vigorous cooperative movement among the small peasants which would greatly facilitate the drive for expanding production on their holdings.

III

An increase in total agricultural output at 4 per cent *per annum* would provide adequate supplies of food grains, oil seeds, sugar cane and cotton to sustain an annual rise of 5 per cent in national income. Nor does the expansion of the corresponding production of manufactures raise any difficult problems. Thus, in addition to food grains, adequate supplies of vegetable oil, sugar (mostly in the form of *gur*) and cotton cloth could be made available. The consumption of all necessities would increase by about 4 per cent *per annum*, which seems to be in proper relation to the rate of growth of national income.

Even though adequate facilities for manufacturing necessities (as for instance, cotton cloth) are provided by the plan, the problem of full utilisation of these facilities may arise. Should a semi-monopolistic increase in prices take place, the demand for the product in question will be restrained and the capacity will not be used to the full extent. The consequences will thus not differ from those of physical shortage. Thus, in addition to making provision for an adequate capacity of produce, control over the prices of necessities will have to be exercised. On the other hand, it should be noted that price control without adequate facilities for production does not solve the problem of supply of necessities at stable prices. Indeed, such a situation is characterized by shortages, haphazard distribution and black markets (unless, of course, comprehensive rationing is introduced, which seems unlikely to function properly in a country like India).

IV

Let us now turn to the second basic problem, namely, that of restraining the consumption of non-essentials to provide sufficient resources for financing of investment. The third five year plan involves an increase in the relative share of home financed investment in the national income, approximately, from 8 per cent in 1960–1 to 12 per cent in 1965–6. If, however, consumption is not restrained by taxation, the rate of saving is not likely to increase significantly. It is true that to the rate of increase in the national income of 5 per cent *per annum* there would be a corresponding annual rise in the consumption of necessities of only 4 per cent. However, this would be made up by a higher rate of increase in the consumption of non-essentials so that total consumption would expand approximately *pari passu* with the national income. To enable the rate of saving to increase from 8 per cent to 12 per cent in the course of the third five year plan, the rate of increase in non-essential consumption should be kept down to approximately 4 per cent *per annum*. Thus it should not exceed the rate of increase in the consumption of necessities which it certainly will, if not restrained by taxation.

The necessary curtailment of expenditure on non-essentials could be achieved most equitably by an increase in the progressive income tax. Unfortunately, apart from taxation of salary earners, the income tax is very ineffective in India because of widespread evasion. However, the existing income tax may be supplemented by direct taxes which could not be easily evaded and which would also in part perform functions other than those of restraining the consumption of non-essentials. The most important of such taxes is the progressive land tax whose effect on agrarian conditions in a direction beneficial to the development of agriculture was outlined above. Next may be mentioned the tax on agricultural rents. Further, the profits on imported articles should be intercepted by means of raising the duties up to the level of the difference between the actual internal market price and the import price. Finally, taxes on commercial premises, factory buildings, and high class residential buildings may be considered which would stimulate, *inter alia*, a more intensive use of the existing space in trade and industry while economising on new construction, and help restrict the building of luxury apartments.

However, the above taxes cannot by any means be expected to restrain non-essential consumption to the extent postulated above. The problem has to be solved to a substantial degree by means of additional excises and duties on selected non-essentials.

In order to put into proper perspective the problem of curtailment of the consumption of non-essentials, it is useful to say a few words on the importance of this consumption as compared with the expenditure on necessities.

A preliminary inquiry into this subject was carried out at my suggestion by the Perspective Planning Division of the Planning Commission. In the expenditure on necessities were included the following items: food grains, potatoes, spices, vegetable oil, hydrogenated oil and *ghee*, *gur* and sugar, fluid milk and *dahi*, sea fish, salt, cotton-cloth, soap, soft coke, firewood and dung, kerosene oil, matches, housing, transport and communication. It should be noted that each item was evaluated at the price of low grade varieties: the value of rice was obtained by multiplying the tonnage by the price of coarse rice; cloth was evaluated similarly by multiplying the yardage by the price of coarse cloth; for fats was substituted a vegetable oil equivalent and for sugar a *gur* equivalent; finally, by the same token, the expenditure on housing, transport and communication was not fully included in necessities. It is clear that in this way the price differentials between higher and lower variety of the respective items were classified as a part of non-essential consumption.

The result of the enquiry is rather striking; it appears that necessities in the above sense constitute only about 55 per cent of the consumer expenditure on goods and services, so that about 45 per cent falls in the category of non-essentials. On this basis, the required reduction in the expenditure on non-essentials in 1965–6 as compared with what it would be otherwise is of the order of 10 per cent. As mentioned above, even after such a curtailment, non-essential consumption would still increase from 1960–1 to 1965–6 at about the same rate as consumption of necessities (i.e., by about 4 per cent *per annum*).

V

Assuring an adequate supply of necessities and restraining the expenditure on non-essentials to the extent necessary for financing of investment are, as said above, the two basic prerequisites of financial stability. It should be noted that the fulfilment of these two conditions does not exclude financing of government investment by loans. Indeed, it appears that even after the introduction of the taxes suggested above, private saving will appreciably exceed planned private investment (as is the case at present). This difference is to be absorbed by public projects and to this extent it will be necessary for government to finance its investment expenditure by loans.

In this connexion it is sometimes asked: How can government 'get hold' of private savings in order to use them for financing of investment? The question is wrongly framed. One should ask rather: How can government restrain private investment to the level allocated to it in the plan? If government succeeds in this private savings over and above private investment may be absorbed by government investment without causing inflationary pressures (of course, on the assumption that the supplies of necessities are adequate and the consumption of non-essentials is appropriately restrained). The absorption of private savings by government investment will proceed automatically. Indeed, to the extent to which this does not happen by direct purchase of government securities, the savings will manifest themselves as increases in the indebtedness of the banking system, inclusive of the Reserve Bank, to the private sector (i.e. the increase in the excess of cash and deposits held by the private sector over banking credits granted to that sector). The counterpart to these savings is the increase in indebtedness of the Government to the banking system. It is in this way that the government 'gets hold' of private savings through this system.

As to the problem of checking the excessive buoyancy of private investment, a variety of methods may be applied: taxes, such as referred to above, and others devised specially for this purpose (rather than for the sake of curtailment of non-essential consumption); selective restrictions on bank credit; and last, but not the least, direct measures such as licensing— all come into consideration and may supplement each other.

VI

It follows from the above that no inflationary pressures will appear under the following conditions:

(*a*) The supply of necessities is in proper relation to a given level of national income.

(*b*) The expenditure on non-essentials is sufficiently restrained to provide out of this level of national income adequate savings for financing of private and government investment;

(*c*) Private investment is sufficiently restrained to leave an adequate part of private savings for financing government investment.

Indeed the problem of avoiding inflationary pressures in economic development is not 'monetary'. It is solved by assuring, by a variety of methods, a correct structure of national expenditure.

10

Hypothetical Outline of
the Five Year Plan
1961–5 for the
Cuban Economy*

❋

INTRODUCTION

This outline of a five year plan of economic development of the Cuban economy for the period 1961–5 is highly hypothetical in character. Any long run plan is based on certain assumptions, which may or may not in fact be fulfilled. What, however, is presented below rests on very flimsy foundations in every possible respect and this is for the following reasons.

(*a*) The statistics of the base period are highly inadequate. In many instances, they are non-existent, or incomplete. Those available are frequently unreliable or presented in a form which makes their utilisation very difficult. Not only quantitative but also qualitative information is scattered in various offices, institutes, etc., and is very difficult to come by.

(*b*) As a result, it is in particular impossible to produce material balances for important items without conducting

* In this work Kalecki was assisted by O. Fernández Balmaceda of FAO (United Nations), E. Fernández Conde, M. Figueras, C. Font, A. Hernández, R. Hernández, F. Lancís, D. Madrazo and J. Pérez de Moral, of *Junta Central de Planificación*, who supplied the basic data and estimates. The five year plan for agriculture on which the present plan is partly based was prepared by Mr. Jacques Chonchol, of FAO (United Nations). The Cuban Government did not accept Kalecki's suggestions for only recently did it introduce five year planning. Mimeographed, December 1960, 45pp.

basic enquiries. Such material balances are, however, a pre-requisite of economic planning. It is of paramount importance to establish them as soon as possible. Otherwise the plans for the immediate future (for 1961 or 1962) will be devoid of any solid foundations, which may have very unpleasant consequences.

(*c*) Long run plans exist only for some sectors of the economy, e.g., textiles, paper, chemical industries and the generation of electricity. At my suggestion Mr. Chonchol has now produced a five year plan for agriculture. There are no plans whatsoever for mining, food, leather, footwear, building materials and engineering industries.

In these circumstances, the purpose of the present enquiry is merely to substantiate the feasibility, under certain conditions, of a high rate of increase in output and consumption, which will lead to the elimination of existing unemployment in the five year period considered and to indicate the changes in the economic structure involved.

The rate of growth postulated here is very high. As will be seen, the national output of goods is to increase at about 13 per cent and consumption of goods at about 10 per cent *per annum*. These rates of growth are much higher than in European socialist countries and they can be achieved only because of certain specific features of the Cuban economy.

(*a*) Cuban agriculture has hitherto been extensive in character. With existing soil and climatic conditions, a rapid intensification at low cost is possible.

(*b*) There exists at present substantial excess capacity in industry and the transport system which reduces the amount of investment required for securing a given rate of growth.

(*c*) The cost of investment is further reduced by climatic conditions, since industrial buildings may be much less sturdy than is the case in a colder climate.

(*d*) This and the relatively high stage of development of construction in Cuba makes for relatively short periods of construction.

While some of these advantages are of a permanent nature (points *c* and *d*), the unutilised resources will to a great extent be exhausted in the course of the execution of the five year plan 1961–5. Thus the rates of growth of this plan must not be extrapolated to the period 1966–70 without further enquiry. It should also be remembered that the rates of growth in question are *averages* for the period 1961–5. It is quite feasible that in the next few years the pace of development will be lower, especially in agriculture where the measures aiming at intensification will not yield results overnight. Therefore the shape of the curve of growth in national output and consumption in the period 1961–5 also requires thorough analysis and no simple interpolation is permissible.

It has been mentioned above that a high rate of growth is possible only if certain conditions are fulfilled. One of them is an expansion of exports of sugar, which is indispensable to provide adequate foreign exchange for the imports required. As will be seen, it is assumed that sugar exports will expand from 1960 to 1965 by about 60 per cent, mainly on account of Soviet and Chinese purchases. The other two conditions I have in mind are, broadly speaking, problems of managing the economy.

First, although the achievement of a leap in agricultural output stands a good chance under Cuban conditions, a considerable organisational effort will be necessary to carry out the intensification required. It is indispensable to draft a full scale programme for the development of agriculture embracing both the government-controlled and the private sector. This programme should include an outline of the economic policies to be pursued with regard to the latter. To implement the programme, the government must provide the agricultural producers with adequate supplies of seeds, fertilisers, machinery, building materials, etc.; it must organise agro-technical assistance; it must directly influence the sector it controls to apply the measures envisaged in the programme and must provide appropriate stimuli for the private sector *inter alia* by purchasing its produce in advance.

The second problem is that of overcoming the scarcity of technicians and skilled workers that is bound to emerge with the postulated rate of growth, especially in newly developed branches of the economy, such as engineering or maritime transport. This problem cannot be solved simply through adequate teaching and training programmes and will require in addition an organised systematic recruitment of foreign technicians.

The development of the Cuban economy now shows a definite tendency towards a higher degree of self-sufficiency. In the present outline of the five year plan, this is reflected in the fact that while national production of goods increases by about 85 per cent, imports hardly exceed the 1958 level. Indeed, in the next five year period, the diversification of the Cuban economy will take the form of a reduction of imports in relation to total demand rather than a diversification of exports, which will continue to be based mainly on sugar, tobacco and minerals.

The tendency towards self-sufficiency is most pronounced in agriculture. The major food imports in 1965 will be confined to wheat, lard and codfish, accounting for only a few per cent of total food consumption. The same tendency will be observed in industry although to a somewhat lesser extent; a high degree of self-sufficiency will be achieved in textiles, paper and chemicals. However, steel production is not likely to be developed on a large scale until 1966 or 1967; the development of the engineering industry will be concentrated mainly on production of durable consumer goods (but not automobiles) and replacement parts for machinery. Thus steel, and its products and machinery, including transport equipment, will continue to be largely imported in 1965. Fuel requirements will also be fully covered by imports.[1]

THE NATIONAL PRODUCT IN 1960

The gross national product of goods and services in 1960 has been estimated in the *Junta Central de Planificación* at about $3,200 million. Of this government and private services constitute about $800 million. Thus national output of goods inclusive of transport and trade would amount to about $2,400 million. The concept of this item corresponds to what is called in the socialist countries national income plus depreciation. Continuing to use the estimates of the *Junta Central de Planificación* we shall split the national output of goods into the values added by the sectors of production shown in Table 1.

TABLE 1

National output of goods in 1960 by sectors

Value added by	$ million	%
Sugar ⎱ (agriculture and manu-	470	19·6
Tobacco ⎰ facturing)	100	4·2
Other agriculture (including fishing and forestry)	430	17·9
Other industry (including energy and construction)	600	25·0
Transport and trade	800	33·3
National output of goods	2,400	100·0

These estimates, although based on shaky foundations, appear to be reasonable when compared with the respective employment figures.

The splitting of the national output of goods in 1960 into investment and consumption is much more difficult. I take investment in fixed capital to be of the order of $500 million in 1960, of which half is in construction and half in equipment. This, however, is a guess rather than an estimate. There is no way even of guessing the value of the change in inventories. Thus when we subtract $500 million of investment in fixed capital from the national output of goods, which is valued at $2,400 million, the remaining part includes, besides personal consumption at retail prices, changes in inventories and also non-investment purchases of goods by the government and by producers of personal services.

TABLE 2

National output of goods in 1960 by destination

Destination	$ million	%
Investment in fixed capital	500	20·8
Consumption of goods, etc.	1,900	79·2
National output of goods	2,400	100·0

PLANNED INCREASE IN NATIONAL OUTPUT OF GOODS
FROM 1960 TO 1965

In Table 3 are given the indices of increases in production of
the sectors into which national output of goods has been split
(see page 159). The index of increase of the national output is
then obtained by weighting the sectorial indices according to
their percentage in this output (see Table 1).

TABLE 3

*Planned increase in the national output of goods
from 1960 to 1965*

Sector	Percentage share in national output 1960 %	Index (1960 = 100)
Sugar	19·6	159
Tobacco	4·2	120
Other agriculture	17·9	188
Other industry	25·0	244
Transport and trade	33·3	165
National output of goods	100·0	186

The basis for the sectorial indices is as follows.

Sugar

It is assumed that exports of sugar in 1965 will be 9 million
tonne (of which about 60 per cent will be to socialist countries
and about 40 per cent to the free market). Allowing for home
consumption, the output in 1965 would be 9·4 million tonne.
In 1960 the output is 5·92 million tonne (including the equivalent of rich molasses and sugar). The index of output (1960 =
100) is thus 159.

Tobacco

It is assumed that both home consumption and exports will
increase by 20 per cent. For home consumption, this means a

per capita increase of 15 per cent *per annum*, which is reasonable in view of the high present consumption of tobacco in Cuba. For exports only a moderate increase should be assumed, for the following reasons. The increase in exports can be achieved only by producing and exporting Virginia tobacco. It will take time to establish a position in the market. On the other hand, maintenance of the present exports of Cuban tobacco to the USA is not quite certain.

Other Agriculture
The index for final product in 1965 in relation to 1960 calculated by Mr. Chonchol on the basis of the five year plan is 186 (see below). This does not include fishing, where production for home consumption and exports may be assumed to triple from 1960 to 1965.[2] On this account, the index has to be increased somewhat, as we consider agriculture jointly with fishing. On the other hand, as we deal with *net* production of particular sectors of the economy the rapid increase in the value of fertilizers used (more than three times) requires a correction in the opposite direction. *Per saldo* we obtain an index of 188 for the net production of agriculture and fishing.

Other Industry (including Energy and Construction)
The index of 244 (1960 = 100) is derived from the plans for particular industries discussed below (see pages 168–75).

Transport and Trade
The main cargo in internal transport is sugar, whose index of production is 159. The index of the joint value of other agriculture, other industry and imports is somewhat over 170. Thus the index of internal transport will be somewhat over 160. The index of trade will differ little from that of consumption which, as will be seen on the next page, is 162. As trade has a much higher value than transport we can safely use this index for total internal transport and trade. We still have to allow for maritime transport. This is very small in 1960, while in 1965 its value added will be something like $20 million (see pages 177–8). As a result, the index for all transport and trade has to be raised to 165.

The index of national output of goods, which is a weighted average of sectorial indices, appears to be 186 (1960 = 100) and its percentage increase *per annum* is about 13 per cent. As the national output of goods has been estimated at $2,400 million the national output in 1965 at 1960 prices would thus amount to $4,460 million.

The value of goods at the disposal of the national economy in 1965 may differ from this figure for two reasons. First, it may be greater than the output on account of foreign credits. We assume, however, that the balance of goods and services in 1965 will be in equilibrium. A possible accrual of credits is treated as a reserve in foreign trade. Next, there is the problem of a change in the terms of trade. The national output in 1965 is calculated at 1960 prices. However, the volume of imported goods, i.e. their value at 1960 prices, may differ from the value of exports at these prices if the price relations change. Thus to obtain from the value of national output the value of goods at the disposal of the economy, the change in terms of trade has to be allowed for. Now, there is a loss in the value of Cuban exports of sugar in 1965 because in 1960 the average price is 3·86 cents per lb, while for 1965 only 3 cents per lb is assumed, as a result of the cessation of exports to the USA. There are also some price reductions on the import side. However, they are smaller, *inter alia* because goods which were bought at very high prices in the USA, for instance rice, no longer enter the list of imports in 1965 because of the development of home production. The main price decreases appear in oil. However, oil was already imported at lower prices in the second half of 1960 and this considerably reduces the importance of the correction. On balance, there is a deterioration by about $150 million (see pages 191–2). Thus goods at the disposal of the economy in 1965 may be valued at $4,310 million ($4,460 million less $150 million).

This amount consists of two components.

(*a*) Investment in fixed capital.

(*b*) Consumption, changes in inventories and non-investment goods purchased by the government and producers of services.

Since investment in fixed capital in 1965 is estimated below (see pages 180–2) at $1,240 million, the other component amounts to $3,070 million ($4,310 million less $1,240 million).

The division of the value of goods at the disposal of the economy between investment and other uses in 1960 and 1965 is shown in Table 4. The last item in the table consists, as said above, of personal consumption, changes in inventories and purchases of non-investment goods by the government and producers of services. However, the bulk of it is certainly consumption and the index 162 can be taken as an approximate measure of its increase. The annual rate of growth is about 10 per cent and since the population is expected to rise at 2·3 per cent *per annum* the rate of increase in *per capita* consumption is about 7·5 per cent.

TABLE 4

National output of goods by destination in 1960 and 1965

	1960 $ million	1965 $ million	Index (1960 = 100)
National output of goods	2,400	4,460	186
Change in terms of trade	—	− 150	
Goods at the disposal of national economy	2,400	4,310	180
Investment in fixed capital	500	1,240	248
Consumption, etc.	1,900	3,070	162

We shall next consider the hypothesis of development for agriculture and industry on which the above estimates are largely based.

PLANNED INCREASE IN AGRICULTURAL PRODUCTION FROM 1960 TO 1965

Mr. Chonchol, who prepared the plan for agriculture, will submit a detailed report on the subject and, therefore, only the salient features of the plan are given here. The increase in the production of the main items, as well as general indices of crop production, animal husbandry and the total final agricultural production, excluding sugar and tobacco, are given in Table 5.

163

TABLE 5

Increase in agricultural production other than
sugar and tobacco from 1960 to 1965

	Index (1960 = 100)
Rice	189
Vegetables and fruit	257
Total crop production	201
Beef	155
Milk	167
Pork	218
Total animal husbandry	175
Total final agriculture production	186

The index of crop production also reflects the introduction of new crops, such as oil seeds and cotton. The increases in agricultural production provide for full self-sufficiency in rice, oil seeds and vegetables, and for a surplus of meat which will make possible exports of beef. The only significant food items of which imports will continue to be made are wheat and lard. However, imports of the latter will be below the present level despite the increase in demand for fats; this will result from production of oil seeds and from expansion of pig rearing. The production of cotton is to satisfy 90 per cent of home consumption.

In addition to self-sufficiency, the plan aims at an improvement of the pattern of nutrition. The relative share of vegetables and fruit in food consumption is to increase considerably; in the composition of the consumption of fats there is to be an important shift from lard to vegetable oils; in the consumption of proteins the relative share of beef will fall and that of poultry and eggs will rise considerably.

The crop production provides adequate fodder for pigs and cows in terms of maize, *millo*, *malanga*, *yucca*, etc. In addition, however, there will be required such protein fodder as the by-products of slaughter-houses, fish meal, final molasses and yeast, which will be produced at home, and oil cakes which will have to be partly imported.

The total area of pastures and land under cultivation is to remain virtually unchanged. However, the area under cultivation is to rise considerably at the expense of pastures. All this increase will be in the non-sugar crops, as the area under sugar cane is to diminish slightly. The changes in the utilisation of agricultural land are shown in Table 6.

TABLE 6

Utilisation of agricultural land
in 1960 and 1965

	1960 %	1965 %
Pastures	66	59
Sugar	19	18
Other crops	15	23
Total agricultural land	100	100

The plan entails a three-fold increase in the use of fertilisers. Except for potassium oxide, the demand will be fully covered by the domestic chemical industry.

The following notes provide some details about the way in which the increase in the production of the main items is to be achieved.

Rice
The increase in production is to be effected through an expansion of the area of cultivation by about 20 per cent and an increase in the yield by 58 per cent. The latter is to be achieved mainly by:

(*a*) Application of fertilisers;
(*b*) Abolishing the cultivation of non-irrigated land and expanding that of irrigated land at present used as pastures;
(*c*) Improving the irrigation through levelling of land,

which for certain varieties of rice will make double cropping possible.

Vegetables

In the case of tomatoes, the increase will mainly be the result of the expansion of the area of cultivation. In the case of other vegetables, the increase in the yield will be of prime importance. It will be achieved through application of fertilisers, improvement in seeds and better cultivation.

Beef

Livestock and the amount slaughtered are to be increased by about 20 per cent and the average net weight of the animals slaughtered by 29 per cent. The improved feeding of the larger number of animals is to be achieved through planting of *pangola* (which provides proper fodder during the dry season), storage of hay, rotation of animals in the pastures and application of fertilisers. All these measures will increase the yield of feeding units per acre to such an extent that it will be possible to fulfil the task of increasing production of beef by 55 per cent and at the same time to reduce the acreage of pastures.

Milk

The proportion of dairy cows to total cattle remains unchanged at 33 per cent, so that their stock increases by about 20 per cent. However, the number of cows milked is to increase more rapidly, namely by 28 per cent. The milk yield per cow is to increase by 31 per cent. This increase will largely be based on the concentrated fodder referred to in the preceding paragraph (grain, oil cakes, molasses). As contrasted with the raising of cattle for slaughter, where concentration is advisable, the dairy cattle should be scattered in various types of farms including small holdings. (One aspect of this is the provision of manure for cultivation.)

Pork

The stock of pigs is to increase by 70 per cent. The rotation is to be somewhat accelerated so that the increase in slaughter is to rise by 90 per cent. At the same time, the net weight of the animals slaughtered is to be 15 per cent higher. The increase in livestock here naturally plays a much greater role than in the production of beef and milk. As pigs will be raised both for pork and lard, *malanga, yucca*, etc. will play an important part in their feeding. These, of course, will have to be supplemented by grain, oil cakes, slaughter-house by-products and fish meal. In raising pigs, the role of small peasants should be even more important than in the production of milk. Indeed, on small farms, pigs can be partly fed on kitchen refuse; moreover, *malanga, yucca*, etc. lend themselves to cultivation in small units. In fact, pig rearing is one of the best methods of intensification of small farms.

Sugar

The increase in the production of sugar, which is not shown in Table 5, is planned at 59 per cent (see page 160). Although the area under sugar cane is to be reduced somewhat (see page 165), the area from which the cane is cut is to increase by 7 per cent, as the proportion of unutilised acreage will decline from 16 to 5 per cent. In order to achieve the planned increase in production, the yield will have to be nearly 50 per cent higher. This will be achieved by planting cane every 5–6 years and by an increased input of fertilisers.

The above plan of development for Cuban agriculture seems to me quite reasonable, but not an easy task to carry out. The plan makes adequate provision for fodder and fertilisers; by this, however, the problem is by no means solved. It is not sufficient to provide enough fertilisers; it is also necessary to handle them competently. For instance, fish meal is excellent protein fodder but skill and experience are necessary to feed it in such a way that the pork does not smell or taste of fish. It also takes a considerable organisational effort to extract from an acre of pasture a yield of feeding units increased to the extent postulated in the plan. From a purely technical point of view, an army of agro-technicians, agricultural instructors, veterinary surgeons, etc. are necessary. But even this is not all, because the most difficult problem is that of management.

The two most important sectors of Cuban agriculture are state farms (administered with the cooperation of the workers' representatives) and the private sector. The latter cannot be managed directly but only by means of various stimuli, contracts for the produce, etc. The results of these measures are never quite certain. A continuous watchfulness is necessary, together with adaptation of policies to the situations which arise. But the big farms under direct government control also raise difficult problems. It is by no means easy to find a skilful managing personnel for a big farm, especially when they do not face a routine job but are to introduce new techniques; and the bigger the farm, the more formidable is the task of management. This should not be construed as a criticism of the system of state farms. On the contrary, in Cuban conditions it would not make sense to split them into peasant holdings. I think only that a single state farm should not be too big a unit and that no excessive tasks should be imposed upon it.

PLANNED INCREASES IN INDUSTRIAL PRODUCTION OTHER THAN SUGAR AND TOBACCO FROM 1960 TO 1965

As mentioned above, we include in industry production of energy and construction. In Table 5 are given the indices for important industrial groups, based on existing plans or on my own assumptions. The underlying material is briefly described in the subsequent notes. The index of increase in industrial production as a whole is obtained by using the weights estimated in the *Junta Central de Planificación*. The industrial groups taken into consideration cover about 90 per cent of the total net value of industry.

The rather low index for oil refining is due to the fact that an increase in refining and imports of crude oil is assumed only up to the point where light oils cover internal demand. The deficiency in heavy oils, the demand for which increases much more quickly than for light oils, is assumed to be covered by imports of fuel oil and gas oil. The large increase in the production of textiles in relation to that of clothing reflects the fact that almost full self-sufficiency is to be achieved in textiles in the period considered, while in clothing this is already the position. The tendency towards full or higher self-sufficiency also affects the indices for food processing (food consumption will increase

TABLE 7

Planned increase in industrial production from 1960 to 1965

Industrial group	Weight %	Index (1960 = 100)
Food processing	13·6	230
Beverages	8·8	160
Clothing and shoes	5·7	170
Textiles	5·2	290
Paper	3·7	390
Chemicals	6·1	240
Oil refining	6·7	130
Electricity	11·1	210
Metals and engineering	7·8	430
Construction and construction materials	26·7	250
Mining	4·6	280
Total	100·0	244

only by about 50 per cent), paper, chemicals and engineering.

The notes on industrial groups given below explain the derivation of the indices of Table 7 and also supply the data on investment required. These provide one of the elements necessary for the estimation of total investment (see page 178).

Food Processing
The index of increase in agricultural production, other than sugar and tobacco (including fishing), is 188 (see page 161). The expansion of food processing must be greater, mainly on account of the production of conserves. This must increase very rapidly, especially if it is taken into consideration that the production of vegetables, fruit and fish for home consumption and for exports will increase 2·5–3 times. We assume for food processing an index of 230. There is considerable excess capacity in the food processing industry, so relatively little investment is required. However, investment is certainly necessary in milk distribution and pasteurisation, where it is estimated that about

$10 million is required, and in the production of conserves. Total investment will probably not exceed $40 million.

Beverages
These are mainly beer and soft drinks. We assume an index of 160 which corresponds to an index of total consumption of goods of 162. According to the survey of family budgets, these items show a somewhat lower increase in demand with a rise in incomes. There also seems to be a considerable excess capacity and no investment has been allowed for.

Clothing and Footwear
On the basis of the family budgets, an index of 170 is assumed in line with prospective increases in demand. As mentioned on page 168, nearly full self-sufficiency exists at present. Considerable excess capacity also exists here and no investment is taken into consideration.

Textiles
In this case, it was possible to utilise the study of Carlos Quintana and Octavio A. Martínez. Mr. Martínez made a new calculation corresponding to the presently assumed rate of increase in total consumption. The figures of production of fabrics and yarn are given for 1959, 1962 and 1965. Interpolating between 1959 and 1962, estimates for 1960 were obtained. The indices for 1965 in relation to 1960 appear to be 280 for fabrics and 300 for yarn. The index for total value added in the textile industry is estimated at 290. This increase is adequate to create near self-sufficiency in textiles, except for jute sacks. But even in the latter sector, where nearly all supplies are at present imported, domestic production from *kenaf* is to cover a significant part of demand. The increase in textile production is to be effected through utilisation of excess capacity, replacement of obsolete machinery and new investment. The total investment outlay in the period 1961–5 amounts to $75 million, of which about $50 million is for machinery.

Paper
The study by Jonko Koljonen and Mario Filippi is utilised here.

The index of the increase in net output from 1960 to 1965 may be estimated at about 390. This will enable the paper industry to cover practically the full demand for paper and cardboard in 1965. The new production is based to a higher degree than hitherto on the use of *bagasse* pulp. This reduces the demand for the imports of other raw materials and contributes to the increase of net output. All the increase is based on new investment: that carried out at present and that anticipated for the period 1961–5. The latter, including a factory for *bagasse* pulp, amounts to about $50 million, of which about $45 million is for machinery.

Chemicals
Only items for which long run plans exist have been considered. These are sulphuric acid, caustic soda, fertilisers, industrial gases, soap and detergents, rayon, explosives and synthetic rubber. In all of these goods, full self-sufficiency will be achieved by 1965 (in soap, rayon and sulphuric acid it already exists). On the basis of the planned increases in production of these items and of material used in their manufacture (estimate of *Junta Central de Planificación*) the aggregate value added has been calculated for 1959 and 1965. The index of increase appears to be 280. For the period 1960–5 this index is estimated at 240. The increase is to be achieved partly by a higher degree of utilisation of the existing capacity; such is, for instance, the case in the production of sulphuric acid and rayon. On the other hand, some branches are to be newly set up, for instance, nitrogen fertilisers. The total investment required is estimated at $75 million, of which $60 million is in machinery.

Oil Refining
The index is based on a study done by the *Junta Central de Planificación*. We assume that no light oils are to be exported in 1965, because it will be difficult to find a market for them. The demand for light oils for 1965 is estimated at about 1·3 million tonne (in terms of the thermic equivalent of crude oil). Assuming the same relation to heavy oils as prevails at present, we obtain for production of heavy oils about 3·9 million tonne (in crude oil equivalent); thus the production of light and heavy

oils requires altogether 5·2 million tonne of crude oil. The actual demand for heavy oils in 1965 is estimated at 6·0 million tonne, so that 2·1 million tonne will have to be imported, in addition to 5·2 million tonne of crude oil. The oil refined in 1960 is estimated at 4·0 million tonne. Thus on the above assumption the index for oil refining is 130 and the absolute increment 1·2 million tonne. The investment corresponding to this increment is about $30 million, of which about $20 million is in equipment and $10 million in construction. It is possible that imports of heavy oils in the quantities mentioned will encounter difficulties. It will then be necessary to expand the refining capacity on a larger scale and make an effort to export the excess gasoline. Another possibility should be mentioned; the pit (*turba*) deposits which have not been sufficiently explored may provide a basis for generation of electricity. In such a case, the demand for imports of fuel oil would be accordingly reduced.

Production of Electricity
The demand for electricity in 1965 has been estimated by the *Junta Central de Planificación* at 5·7 GWh. I have tried to check this estimate by a comparison with Poland, taking into consideration the levels of national income and the structure of industry and in the light of this comparison the estimate seems reasonable. The demand in 1960 is estimated at about 2·7 GWh, so that the index of increase is about 210. The necessary investment is estimated at $245 million, of which machinery and the network amount to about $220 million and construction to $25 million.

Engineering
I have received no data on this industry and have had therefore to improvise. I assume that, in view of the lack of technicians and skilled workers, the development of the industry has to be confined mainly to the manufacture of durable consumer goods (except automobiles) and replacement parts, in order to reduce imports of these two items. This, especially the manufacturing of replacement parts, will also provide a training ground for skilled workers. In this way, a sound basis will be provided for

a rapid development of machinery proper after 1965. The index of increase is calculated in the following way. The value added in 1960 corresponding to the weight of the industry adopted for the calculation of the index of industrial production (see Table 7) is $42 million. This item consists mainly of repairs, and production of some replacement parts, implements, etc. We assume these activities to increase proportionately to national output of goods, i.e. in the proportion of 1·86; in addition, however, we assume that the industry will cover two-thirds of the demand for durable consumer goods and two-thirds of the replacement parts and implements at present imported. The demand for durable consumer goods in 1965 is estimated on the following basis.

(*a*) The total value of consumption of goods in 1960 and its increase up to 1965.

(*b*) The relative share of durable goods made of metal in consumption according to family budgets.

(*c*) The elasticity of demand for such durable goods in relation to the total demand for goods.

We arrive at about $90 million as the value of consumption of durable goods made of metal in 1965 at retail prices, or about $75 million at wholesale prices. Of these two-thirds are to be covered by new production. The imports of replacement parts and implements are assumed to be about $70 million in 1960 (see page 181). We assume that the demand for these items is to increase proportionately to the rise of national output of goods, i.e. by 86 per cent in five years. Thus we estimate this demand at $130 million. Again two-thirds of this are to be covered by the new production. Moreover, we estimate the value added in the manufacture of durable goods and replacement parts at 75 per cent of their actual value. We can now estimate the value of engineering industry in 1965 (see Table 8).

The absolute increase in the value of production thus amounts to about $140 million. I may venture a guess that the investment required to achieve this increment will not exceed $100 million.

Construction and Construction Materials
The value of total construction is to increase, according to the estimate of investment, from $250 million in 1960 to $620

TABLE 8

Estimated value of engineering industry in 1965

	$ million
'Old types' of production in 1965	$42 \times 1\cdot86 = 78$
'New production' of durable goods	$0\cdot66 \times 75 \times 0\cdot75 = 38$
'New production' of replacement parts, etc.	$0\cdot66 \times 130 \times 0\cdot75 = 65$
Engineering production in 1965	181
Engineering production in 1960	42
Index 1965 (1960 = 100)	430

million in 1965 (see Table 13). Accordingly, we estimate the joint index of construction and construction materials in 1965 at about 250 (1960 = 100). Investment in construction equipment is estimated at $80 million. Investment in cement production, which is the main building material, can be evaluated as follows. The demand for cement in 1965 is estimated on the basis of the volume and the structure of construction in that year at 1·5 million tonne. The present maximum capacity is about 1 million tonne. To allow for some reserves and for other uses of cement in construction we shall assume a capital outlay corresponding to 0·75 million tonne. This amounts to about $30 million, of which about $25 million is for equipment.

Mining

We estimate the value of mining production in 1960 at the level of 1958 exports, which was about $28 million. For 1965, we assume that the value of production from 'old' mines will achieve the level of exports in 1957, which is the highest in recent years, i.e. about $35 million. In addition, we take into consideration the production of nickel concentrates from the Moa plants valued at $37 million. We do not deduct from this the value of sulphuric acid produced in the plant for internal use, because it is not included in the chemical industry, but merely the necessary imports of sulphur of about $4 million, which leaves $33 million. We assume, moreover, that the production of iron ore from deposits ascertained by Soviet geologists will achieve a level of 1 million tonne *per annum*, the value of which is about $10 million. In 1965, the steel plant, whose construction is planned, will not yet be in operation, so that the iron ore will be exported. The total mining production would thus amount to $78 million and the index of mining for 1965 to about 280 (1960 = 100).

Steel

As said above, the new plant will be in operation only after 1965 (probably in 1966 or 1967). The present small plant may be utilised to a much higher degree than at present. However, the value added would remain so small that this need not be taken into consideration in our discussion. This is the reason why the steel industry is not listed in Table 7. As concerns investment in the new plant, however, it will to a large extent be incurred before 1965 and therefore it must be included in our estimates for the period 1961–5. The Soviet credit granted for equipment amounts to $100 million. It will not be fully used in the period considered; on the other hand there will be additional expenditure on construction. We assume that, on balance, the total invesment in the period 1961–5 will be $100 million.

INVESTMENT IN THE PERIOD 1961–5

We shall first estimate productive investment, i.e. that which is necessary in order to achieve the planned increase in the national output of goods in the five year period. Next we shall tackle the unproductive investment in residential building and public construction (schools, hospitals, water supply and sewage, streets and roads, etc.).

Table 9 brings together the estimates of industrial investment given in the preceding section (equipment includes installation costs). As will be noticed, for certain items the split between equipment and building is not available. This was crudely estimated in order to arrive at the respective totals. These estimates of industrial investment are not complete because of numerous omissions. However, all major projects have been taken care of. As will be seen below, we shall add to the total value of productive investment—which we shall estimate, a reserve to provide for the gaps in our estimates.

It should be added that no new investment in sugar mills is required, because the planned increase in production will be achieved through the extension of the period of the *zafra*.

No research has yet been done on investment in agriculture, therefore, only a guess may be ventured. We assume that in the period 1961–5 $500 million will be spent, of which $200 million will be for equipment (tractors and machinery) and $300 million for construction (granaries, warehouses, fences, ditches, etc.).

TABLE 9

Industrial investment in 1961–65

Industry	Equipment $ millions	Construction $ millions	Total $ millions
Food processing	—	—	40
Textiles	50	25	75
Paper	45	5	50
Chemicals (including synthetic rubber)	60	15	75
Oil refining	20	10	30
Electricity	220	25	245
Engineering	70	30	100
Construction	80	—	80
Cement	25	5	30
Steel	—	—	100
Total	670	155	825

Next, we shall estimate investment in transport. It seems fairly certain that considerable excess capacity exists in the transport of goods by railways and trucks, even at the peak during the *zafra* period. If, as assumed above, the increase in the production of sugar is effected by lengthening that period, no extension in the capacity of the transport system seems necessary. We therefore confine investment in this sphere to replacement and some modernisation.

For the railways, this type of investment, excluding maintenance of the truck and repairs of rolling stock which are covered by the subsequent general estimate of maintenance, can be estimated at something like $25 million in the five year period.

For trucks it is assumed that:

(*a*) All the stock of highway trucks, which is rather obsolete, will be replaced in the five year period. This investment amounts to about $25 million (1,600 trucks at $17,000 each);

(*b*) Only 10 per cent of light trucks will be replaced during this time because they wear out more slowly and are in a much better condition at present. This investment also amounts to about $25 million (10 per cent of 42,000 trucks at $6,000 each).

For buses, we assume a replacement of 11 per cent *per annum* and a 5 per cent increase in stock. The stock of buses is at present 5,500 and the cost per unit is $21,000. The outlay required amounts to about $100 million.

The total investment in transport equipment for internal use would thus amount to $175 million in the five year period. Moreover, the construction outlay on bus terminals, airports and harbours is estimated by Mr. Balmaceda at $75 million. We shall still have to estimate the investment in shipping.

It is assumed that the merchant marine will be built up to the level at which cargo is assured on the full round trip because only under such conditions is the investment sufficiently profitable. This excludes investment in oil tankers because they cannot carry sugar (or any other major Cuban exports). The import cargo other than oil in 1965 may be estimated for the items set out in Table 14 at about 2 million tonne. This is much less than exports of sugar and, therefore, it is the import cargo other than oil that sets the limit to the Cuban merchant marine. It would not, however, be safe to assume that it will be possible to manage to bring all this cargo in Cuban ships carrying a full load on every round trip. We assume that it will be possible to do so for up to 70 per cent of the import cargo, i.e. 1·4 million tonne.

Thus, Cuban ships would carry 1·4 million tonne of sugar one way and 1·4 million tonne of non-oil imports on the return trip. It appears that the freight earned on the export of sugar will then cover the cost in foreign exchange of the round trip and the freight paid on 0·6 million tonne of imports brought by foreign ships.

The necessary investment can be estimated as follows. A ship trading between Cuba and a Baltic port will make about eight round trips in a year. Let us take this as the average, because some other trips will be much longer and some much shorter. Thus the merchant marine must have the capacity of carrying $\frac{1·4 \times 10^6}{8} = 175,000$ tonne, which is equivalent to about 190,000 dead weight tonnage. The investment involved amounts to about $55 million. The receipts from operation of the merchant fleet at this capacity net of the current costs in foreign exchange would be about $20 million.

We can now put together all the productive investments estimated above. In view of the incompleteness of our estimates and of the fact that no investment maturing after 1965 (except the steel plant) has been taken into consideration, a reserve of about 20 per cent is added.

TABLE 10

Productive investment (exclusive of current maintenance) in 1961–5

	Equipment $ million	Construction $ million	Total $ million
Industry (including energy and construction)	670	155	825
Agriculture	200	300	500
Internal transport	175	75	250
Shipping	55	—	55
Apparent total	1,100	530	1,630
Reserve	200	100	300
Corrected total	1,300	630	1,930

We shall now estimate the unproductive investment, starting with residential building. The estimate is based on the prospective increase in the urban population and on a standard number of persons per room in new apartments. The total increase in population in the five year period may be estimated at 800,000 (2·3 per cent per year), of which 700,000 may be supposed to accrue to the urban areas. The assumptions about the standard number of persons per room are arrived at as follows.

According to the census of 1953 about 37 per cent of rooms in urban areas fall into the group of apartments of 5 or more rooms. The average in this category is 6 rooms per apartment. These are in most cases apartments of the rather rich population. We assume that the number of persons per room in these apartments is on the average 0·8, which corresponds approximately to 5 persons (inclusive of a servant) in a 6 room apartment. The average number of persons per room for the whole urban population according to the census is 1·3. On this basis, it is possible to determine the number of persons per room in apartments of 4 or fewer rooms. The total number of rooms in these apartments is 100 − 37 = 63 per cent of all rooms. Thus we have

$$(0·37 \times 0·8) - 0·63\,X = 1·3$$

where X denotes the number of persons per room in smaller apartments. We obtain from this equation $X = 1·6$. Thus in the apartments of 4 or fewer rooms there were in 1953 probably 1·6 persons per room. The percentage of population living in these apartments is

$$\frac{0·63 \times 1·6}{1·3} = 77 \text{ per cent.}$$

This means that the standard of the mass of the population in 1953 was about 1·6 persons per room. As living conditions have deteriorated somewhat, we may assume that it is now, say, 1·7 persons per room. This may be considered a minimum standard in the five year period. On this basis, the increase in population by 700,000 requires the building of 411,000 rooms (in all these considerations the kitchen is not considered a room, in line with Cuban statistics). The present building cost of a room is on the average $1,870. However, by various economies it is hoped to reduce the cost by 20 per cent, i.e. to $1,500. Thus the investment required may be estimated at about $620 million.

In addition, we postulate $160 million for residential building in rural areas, slum clearing and repairs. It should be noted that with regard to rural building the amount in question represents only the contribution of the government, to the extent of about 50 per cent of the full value, since it is assumed that the remainder, consisting of labour and bricks produced in a primitive fashion, would be contributed by the peasants themselves. This part is *not* included in the above estimates of investment. Assuming, for instance, that a $100 million would be spent on house building in rural areas, the value of new houses would be $200 million, which would make about 100,000 houses.

The total value of residential building arrived at above is $780 million. The value of other unproductive investment has been estimated by Mr. Balmaceda at $950 million. Its breakdown is shown in Table 11. The total unproductive investment thus amounts to $1,730 million.

TABLE 11

Unproductive investment in 1961–5

Investment	$ million
Schools	175
Public health	70
Other public buildings	50
Roads	385
Parks, sport, tourism	50
Streets	60
Water supply and sewage	160
Total	950
Residential building	780
Total	1,730

We can now put together our estimates for productive and unproductive investment (excluding maintenance in the productive sector) in the five year period.

The estimate of investment in 1965 is given in Table 13. It has been arrived at as follows.

It has been assumed (see page 159) that investment in 1960 amounts to $500 million, of which $250 million is in construction and $250 million in new equipment and maintenance in the productive sector. We now assume, moreover, that of the latter part $110 million was for new equipment (imported) and $140 million for maintenance. This item in turn is assumed to be subdivided into $70 million of imported replacement parts and implements, and $70 million of domestic maintenance (repairs and manufacturing of replacement parts and implements).

TABLE 12

Productive and unproductive investment in 1961–5

	Equipment $ million	Construction $ million	Total $ million
Productive investment	1,300	630	1,930
Unproductive investment	—	1,730	1,730
Total investment	1,300	2,360	3,660

We assume that investment both in construction and new equipment increases linearly from 1960 to 1965. It will easily be seen that the figures $620 million and $360 million given in Table 13 for these two items tally with the respective totals of investment in construction and new equipment as given in Table 12. Indeed, for the six year period the figures in the table yield for construction

$$\left(\frac{250 + 620}{2}\right) 6 = \$2,610 \text{ million}$$

and for the period 1961–5 by subtraction of investment in 1960 we obtain

$$2,610 - 250 = \$2,360 \text{ million,}$$

which agrees with the respective figures in Table 12. In the same way we obtain for equipment

$$\left(\frac{110 + 360}{2}\right) 6 - 110 = \$1,300 \text{ million}$$

in the 1961–5 period, which again agrees with the respective item in Table 12.

Finally, we assume the current maintenance in the productive sector to vary proportionately to the national output of goods.

Thus in 1965 this item is higher than in 1960, in the proportion 1·86, and amounts to $260 million.

It may be added that the current maintenance, which varies throughout the period in proportion to the national output of goods, amounts in the whole five year period to about $1,030 million. Thus total investment inclusive of current maintenance in that period amounts in accordance with Table 12 to about $4,700 million.

TABLE 13

Investment (inclusive of current maintenance) in 1960 and 1965

	1960 $ million	1965 $ million
Construction	250	620
New equipment	110	360
Current maintenance*	140	260
Total	500	1,240

* In the productive sector; includes also implements.

FOREIGN TRADE IN 1965

In Table 14 imports and exports in 1965 are given by single items. As no foreign credits have been assumed (see page 162) an equilibrium in the balance of trade can in principle be expected. Indeed, the production of goods available for export must in such a case be adequate to cover imports. Such is, however, in practice, the case only if the plan is based on commodity balances from which can be derived the imports required and the surpluses available and suitable for exports. As the present outline of the plan is very loosely constructed the discrepancy between imports and exports in Table 10 is surprisingly small. The basis of the estimates of single import and export items is set out below. However, before proceeding with these explanations it may be useful to make a few observations on the nature of the assumptions about foreign trade in 1965 as presented in Table 14.

TABLE 14

Imports and exports in 1965 at f.o.b. prices

Imports	$ million	Exports	$ million
Durable consumption		Sugar	585
goods	40	Final molasses	30
Automobile and parts	25	Tobacco	60
Wheat	25	Coffee	20
Lard	16	Vegetable and fruits	7
Codfish and sardines	8	Fruit, conserves and	
Other food and drink	8	sweets	15
Drugs	20	Fish	10
Metals and products	77	Net exports of meat	26
Timber	12	Minerals	82
Machinery and parts	353		
Crude and heavy oils	80		
Textiles and materials	25		
Oil cakes	10		
Wood pulp	10		
Materials for breweries	5		
Materials for chemical			
industry	24		
Jute sacks	14		
Other goods	70		
Total merchandise		Total merchandise	
imports	822	exports	835
Net freight paid on			
imports	33	Discrepancy	20
Total	855	Total	855

It will be noticed that imports of merchandise in 1965 differ little from the 1958 level ($822 million as against $777 million) despite the increase of about 90 per cent in the national output of goods from 1960 to 1965. This, as already mentioned, reflects the increase in the self-sufficiency of the economy. It is in this way that the economy will be diversified, because the structure of exports does not undergo any substantial change, the main items continuing to be sugar and by-products, tobacco and minerals, which together constitute about 90 per cent of total exports.

On the import side the largest single items are machinery, fuel and metals (mainly steel), together amounting to about 55 per cent of total imports. These are all items in which the degree of self-sufficiency in 1965 will still continue to be low.

The following notes explain how the particular *import* items have been estimated.

Durable Consumer Goods

The total demand for goods made of metal was estimated on page 173 at $75 million at wholesale prices, of which one-third, i.e. $25 million, would be imported and the remainder would be produced at home. To these should be added certain parts of durable goods, which will have to be imported for their manufacture; their value may be estimated at $5 million. The imports of other durable consumer goods are estimated at roughly $10 million.

Automobiles and Parts

In the next few years, the import of automobiles will cease because of import difficulties and because some of the automobiles belonging to the richer population will be disposed of. However, by 1965 replacement and increase in stock, which is assumed to be in proportion to the increase in population, will have to be renewed. We assume a period of replacement of 11 years. With an increase of population of 2·3 per cent *per annum*, imports will amount to 11·3 per cent of the stock. The latter is about 195,000 cars, so that imports would be 22,000 cars. Assuming a small car costs $900, we arrive at $20 million. In addition, we allow $5 million for replacement parts.

Wheat

Imports of wheat and wheat flour, in terms of wheat, in 1958 were about 255,000 tonne. In 1960 consumption may be something like 275,000 tonne. On the basis of the survey of family budgets and the increase in total consumption of goods from 1960 to 1965, the increase in the demand for wheat may be estimated at 27 per cent. No production will be undertaken, but imports will be of grain only (no flour). At a price of $70 per tonne, total imports in 1965 may be estimated at $25 million.

Lard
On the assumption that the plan for production of oil seeds and the raising of pigs will be fulfilled it is necessary according to Mr. Chonchol to import lard worth about $16 million.[3]

Codfish and Sardines
The value of imports in 1958 amounted to about $6 million. We assume for 1965 a value of imports of $8 million. It should be noted that the value of home-produced supplies of fish is to be tripled.

Other Food and Drink
The programme for agriculture makes it possible to eliminate all imports of fruit and vegetables. However, imports of olive oil and wine from Spain are to be stabilised at their 1958 level of $8 million in order to retain the Spanish market for Cuban tobacco.

Drugs
As no inquiry has been made into the development of the production of pharmaceuticals no proper estimate of imports in 1965 can be made. We assume the imports to remain at the 1958 level of about $20 million, which means a much higher degree of self-sufficiency as the demand will increase considerably.

Metals and Products
The estimate is based on a rather hypothetical balance of steel in 1959 prepared in the *Junta Central de Planificación* and on the direct evaluation of steel required for construction planned for 1965 by Mr. Balmaceda. According to the balance for 1959, the consumption of rolled steel, amounting to 143,000 tonne, was split into the following three categories:

(a) Construction—75,000 tonne

(*b*) Tinplate—33,000 tonne
(*c*) Other uses—35,000 tonne.

The value of construction planned for 1965 is about triple the level of 1959. Thus steel used for this purpose in that year may be roughly estimated at 220,000 tonne. Mr. Balmaceda's evaluation yielded 180,000 tonne. As the norms he applied may be on the low side, I adopt the figure of 200,000 tonne. The increase in the use of tinplate will be very high, because of the rapid development of conserves; I postulate for 1965 a volume of 80,000 tonne. The most complex estimate is that of other uses, which I model on that of the engineering industry (see page 173). I split the steel in question into two components:

(*a*) The consumption in the basic period, increased in proportion with the national output of goods as compared with 1959; this would mean about double 35,000 tonne, i.e. 70,000 tonne;

(*b*) The steel required in the manufacture of currently imported durable goods and replacement parts for machinery or implements.

The value (at wholesale prices) of this new production is to be two-thirds of $205 million or about $135 million (see page 173). Assuming steel consumption of about 0·8 tonne of steel per $1,000 we obtain 110,000 tonne. The total consumption of steel in 1965 would thus be:

(*a*) Construction—200,000 tonne.
(*b*) Tinplate—   80,000 tonne.
(*c*) Other uses—$\left\{ \begin{array}{l} \text{70,000 tonne.} \\ \text{110,000 tonne.} \end{array} \right.$
    Total—460,000 tonne.

The value of this at $150 per tonne amounts to $69 million. The home production of steel will contribute something to this, but not much if the imports of raw materials used in this production are deducted from the value of prospective production. On the other hand, we have to allow for the imports of non-ferrous metals. On balance, we adopt a figure of $77 million for the total imports of metals and their products.

Timber

The amount necessary for construction in 1965 has been estimated by Mr. Balmaceda at 280,000 tonne. Projected back to

1958 according to the ratio of the value of construction at the two dates, about 80,000 tonne is arrived at. Imports in 1958 amounted to about 110,000 tonne. Part of the difference may be attributed to the underestimation of investment in 1958 and part to other uses of timber or underestimation of requirements for construction in 1965. It seems reasonable to add, say, 25 per cent to 280,000 tonne in order to arrive at total demand. Thus we arrive at 350,000 tonne. Of these part will be covered by *bagasse*, wood or chipboard, the production of which can easily be expanded (it should be noted that production of these items did not exist in 1958). Assuming 25 per cent of the total demand as the limit for the use of these substitutes the quantity to be imported would be about 260,000 tonne which at a price of $47 per tonne amounts to $12 million.

Machinery and Parts

According to Table 13 investment in machinery proper amounts in 1965 to $360 million. Deducting freight and installation, which make up about 15 per cent of the import price, we arrive at imports at f.o.b. prices of about $310 million. Moreover, it follows from page 173 that machine parts and implements to be imported in 1965 amount to one-third of $130 million or to about $43 million.

Crude Oil and Heavy Oils

According to page 171–2 total imports amount to 5·2 million tonne of crude oil and 2·1 million tonne of heavy oils, or 7·3 million tonne altogether. Valuing it roughly at a price for crude oil (f.o.b. Soviet port) of $11 we arrive at about $80 million.

Textiles and Materials

From the plan for the development of the textile industry it may be estimated that the small quantities of clothing, fabrics (except jute sacks), yarn and raw materials to be imported amount to $25 million.

Oil Cakes

It follows from the balance of fodder (see page 165) that it will be necessary in 1965 to import about 10,000 tonne of oil cakes, at a value of about $10 million.

Wood Pulp
It follows from the plan for the paper industry that in 1965 about 90,000 tonne of wood pulp will be required. In addition, the production of rayon will absorb about 10,000 tonne, so that the total requirements will be about 100,000 tonne. At a price of about $100 per tonne the value of imports amounts to about $10 million.

Materials for Breweries
In 1958, these imports amounted to $2·5 million. In line with the anticipated increase in production of beer we estimate the imports in 1965 at about $5 million.

Materials for Chemical Industries
Only industries for which long run plans exist are taken into consideration here (see page 171), i.e. sulphuric acid, caustic soda, fertilisers, industrial gases, soap and detergents, explosives and synthetic rubber. The imports of materials for these industries amount to about $20 million. We add to this $4 million worth of sulphur for the production of sulphuric acid in the Moa nickel plant for internal use (the value of this production has been included not in the chemical industry, but in mining). Thus total imports are estimated at $24 million.

Jute Sacks
In 1958 about 48,000 tonne were imported. The increase in sugar production by about 60 per cent will raise the requirements to 77,000 tonne. However, by 1965 the production of sacks from *kenaf* will provide 20,000 tonne so that only 57,000 tonne have to be imported. At a price of about $250 per tonne this amounts to about $14 million. If efforts to ship a high proportion of sugar in bulk succeed, the imports required will be accordingly lower.

Other Goods
These are goods the imports of which are neither eliminated nor determined by any of the preceding estimates of agricultural and industrial production in relation to demand. We treat their

imports in the same way as we did in the case of drugs; we assume the imports to remain at the 1958 level despite the increase in total demand, as a result of a higher proportion being covered by home production. As mentioned on page 183, this is also the tendency for total imports which differ little from the 1958 level.

Net Freight Paid on Imports
We have assumed that Cuba will invest in shipping up to a limit of about 70 per cent of the imported cargo except oil. The ships will carry sugar one way and bring import cargo on the return trip. The freight earned on sugar will then approximately cover the costs in foreign exchange of the round trip and the freight on the 30 per cent of imported non-oil cargo brought by foreign ships. Thus we have to charge to the import side only the freight on oil which is imported from the USSR. The import of oil amounts to 7·3 million tonne, which at about $4·5 per tonne makes $33 million.

Below follow notes explaining how the particular *export* items have been estimated.

Sugar
The export of sugar has been assumed to reach a level of 9 million tonne in 1965 (see page 160). Moreover, we assume an export price of 3 cents per lb. Thus the value of exports amounts to about $585 million.

Final Molasses and Products
In 1960 production amounted to 290 million gallons. To estimate the production in 1965, we apply the index of production of sugar which is 159 (see page 160) and obtain about 460 million gallons. In order to arrive at exports we have to evaluate home consumption. We assume that about 100 million gallons were used in 1960 for fuel (as admixture for gasoline or for cookers) and for drinks. For all these uses, a moderate increase, say, of 20 per cent may be assumed up to 1965. The fodder balance in 1965 requires about 30 million gallons of molasses and about 15,000 tonne of yeast. The latter may be obtained as a by-product of alcohol production. Altogether for home use

150 million gallons would thus be required, which would leave 310 million gallons for exports. At 8 cents per gallon, the exports would amount to $25 million. We have abstracted so far from exports of alcohol and yeast, into which additional molasses could be converted. Further research is required to ascertain the possible scale of such an operation. However, it seems safe to add $5 million on this account.

Tobacco
Exports in 1958 amounted to about $50 million. We assume an increase of 20 per cent up to 1965. Our reasons were given above (see page 160).

Coffee
Exports of coffee of about 20,000 tonne are postulated, which is about triple that in 1958. This is based on the exceptional quality of Cuban coffee. At a price of $1,000 per tonne this makes $20 million.

Vegetables and Fruit
Exports of fresh tomatoes, cucumbers, bananas, oranges and pineapples are estimated, in accordance with the plan for agricultural production, at about $7 million. In 1958 these exports amounted to about $4 million.

Fruit Conserves and Sweets
It is postulated that this item, which amounted in 1958 to about $5 million, will be tripled, mainly on account of large increases in exports of pineapple conserves.

Fish
It is postulated that this item, which in 1958 amounted to about $5 million, will be doubled.

Net Exports of Meat
The value of animal agricultural production in the base period is estimated at about $260 million and it is to increase by 75 per cent up to 1965. The total consumption of animal products is assumed to increase in the same proportion as the total con-

sumption of goods, i.e. by 62 per cent. (The assumption is based on the elasticity of demand for animal products in relation to total demand for goods derived from family budgets, which is approximately equal to one.) Thus a surplus of about $34 million would arise at the prices received by producers. This surplus is equivalent to about 54,000 tonne of beef. However, in the base year, about 13,000 tonne of pork were imported and these imports, as part of the total consumption of animal products, would also tend to increase up to 1965 by 62 per cent, i.e. to the level of 21,000 tonne. Thus the net surplus of meat would amount to 33,000 tonne of beef. This, valued at $800 per tonne, gives about $26 million as the net export of meat in terms of beef.

Minerals

The highest exports in the period 1956–9 were about $35 million *per annum* which I take as the measure of productive capacity. This does not include the nickel production of the Moa nickel plant which is to produce in the near future output worth about $37 million. In addition, we assume exports of 1 million tonne of iron ore at a price of about $10 per tonne (see page 175), which makes $10 million.

We have still to estimate the loss resulting from the change in prices of imports and exports between 1960 and 1965 (see page 162). The average export price of sugar in 1960 was 3·86 cents per lb while for 1965 we assume a price of 3 cents per lb. If sugar were exported at 1960 prices, the receipts would thus be higher by 29 per cent, or by $585 million × 0·29 = $170 million. On the import side, the scope of reductions is much less because many goods which were bought at very high prices in the USA (for instance, rice) do not enter 1965 imports as a result of the development of domestic production. Moreover, the difference in prices of oil is reduced by the fact that in the second half of 1960 cheap Soviet oil was already imported. Thus although Venezuelan or US oil was more expensive by about 30 per cent (on a c.i.f. basis), only about 15 per cent must be taken into consideration when the gain in 1965 is compared with 1960. The imports of oil in 1965 amount on a c.i.f. basis to $113 million, so that the gain as compared with the valuation at 1960 prices may be estimated at $17 million. As to other imports, they are, in general, estimated at prices not significantly different from those obtained in 1960. Should they in fact be lower it will be a favourable factor in the balance of trade; however, no adjustment is required on that score for reconciliation between the national product and the balance of trade.

On the balance, such an adjustment, i.e. the deduction from national output of goods necessary in order to arrive at the volume of goods at the disposal of the economy, may be estimated at about $150 million.

EMPLOYMENT

In this section the increase in employment in the main sectors of the economy from 1960 to 1965 is estimated on the assumption of full employment in the latter year. Next, the problems of the increase in real incomes and of changes in productivity and working time during the five year period are examined.

As measures of the labour force and employment for 1960, the data from the enquiry on employment in the period February–July 1960 are adopted. The averages for this period cannot differ much from the annual averages because the seasonal changes in employment between the average of the six months (February–July) and the yearly average are small. In any case, we are interested here in the indices for 1965 in relation to 1960, rather than in absolute values. In Table 15 are given figures for the labour force and employment in 1960 and anticipated figures for the labour force or employment in 1965 (labour force and employment coincide for that year because of the assumption of full employment). We assume that the total labour force will increase 3 per cent *per annum*, slightly more than the population which increases by 2·3 per cent *per annum*, on account of a higher degree of employment of women. We assume, moreover, that the agricultural labour force remains stable over the next five years, so that the whole increase in the total labour force accrues to non-agricultural occupations. Finally, we assume only a moderate increase of 20 per cent in employment in services, on account of the anticipation of a reduction in domestic service.

The divergence between the indices of labour force and employment reflects the process of elimination of unemployment. In addition, however, to unemployment there existed, in the basic period, underemployment in the form of short time work. This underemployment may be estimated from the enquiry referred to above as being of the order of 5 per cent of employment in terms of full labour weeks (i.e. about 5 per cent of full labour weeks in 1960 were lost on account of short time work). As this percentage is similar for all types of employment covered by Table 15, we may obtain the index of employment in full labour weeks in 1965 in relation to 1960 by dividing the last column of Table 15 by 0·95. We then obtain the comparison of the increase in the five year period of the labour force, employment in terms of persons and employment expressed in full labour weeks (see Table 16).

TABLE 15

Labour force and employment in 1960 and 1965

Type of employment	1960 Labour force millions	1960 Employment millions	1965 Labour force or employment millions	1965 Labour force index (1960 =100)	1965 Employment index (1960 =100)
Agriculture	0·86	0·77	0·86	100	112
Non-agri-culture	1·41	1·24	1·76	125	142
Produc-tive	0·93	0·80	1·23	132	154
Services	0·48	0·44	0·53	110	120
Total	2·27	2·01	2·62	116	130

It is now possible to ascertain whether the increase in consumption of 62 per cent arrived at above (see page 163) is adequate to sustain this increase in employment and still leave some room for raising real wages. We may assume, I think, that the aggregate real income (net of tax) in agriculture and non-agriculture should increase in the same proportion. It is true that in agriculture the labour force is to remain unchanged while in other occupations it is to increase by 25 per cent (see Table 16) and thus income per head of the labour force will rise in agriculture by 25 per cent more; but in view of the wide discrepancy between the standard of living of the urban and the rural population in Cuba this seems fully justified.

On this assumption we obtain the indices of supply of consumer goods per full labour week by dividing the index of total supply, i.e. 162, by the indices of full labour weeks as given in Table 16.

TABLE 16

Increases in labour force and employment
from 1960 to 1965

Type of employment	Labour force	Employment indices (1960 = 100)	
		in persons	in full labour weeks
Agriculture	100	112	118
Non-agriculture	125	142	150
Productive	132	154	162
Services	110	120	126
Total	116	130	137

These results are of considerable importance. The increase in the supply of consumer goods in the non-agricultural sector is only 8 per cent, so that hardly any margin is left for an increase in real wages in this sector. The large increase in aggregate consumption is almost fully absorbed by the elimination of unemployment and underemployment, as well as by a considerable increase in the real income of agricultural workers and peasants. It is true that consumption per head of the non-agricultural labour force increases by 30 per cent. However, this happens mainly by abolishing unemployment, which politically is by no means equivalent to a straight increase of real wages by 30 per cent.

One solution of the problem would be to have a higher rate of increase of national income and consumption. I consider, however, that even the present plan is by no means easy to carry out. Another solution would be to limit the rate of increase in rural incomes. This again seems to me inadvisable, the more so in that it would yield relatively little for an increase in urban wages, just because rural consumption in the base period is relatively low. There definitely exists a serious political problem here, which must be taken into consideration. Perhaps it is relevant to this point that, as will be seen below, it will probably be necessary to reduce working hours in order to achieve full employment. This would, of course, leave unchanged the real income per worker, as determined above by the fully employed labour force and the supply of consumer goods. But it would increase the *hourly* wage in inverse proportion to the shortening of working time.

TABLE 17

Supply of consumer goods per head of labour force and per full labour week in 1965 in relation to 1960

Consumer goods	Indices (1960 = 100)		
	aggregate	per head of labour force	per full labour week
Agriculture	162	162	137
Non-agriculture	162	130	108
Total	162	140	118

We shall now determine the changes in productivity in the agricultural and non-agricultural sectors, by comparing the increases in the production of goods by these sectors with the respective increases in employment in terms of full labour weeks. For this purpose, we still have to split the national output into agricultural and non-agricultural components. We have not done this yet, because sugar and tobacco were treated as entities without splitting them between agricultural and industrial production. It appears that while the total national output of goods and services is to increase from 1960 to 1965 by 86 per cent, the increases for agricultural and non-agricultural sectors are approximately 75 and 90 per cent, respectively. These increases are compared with the increases in full employment in terms of labour weeks, as given in Table 16, of 18 per cent for agriculture and 62 per cent for the productive sector of non-agriculture (we do not include employment in services because they do not enter the national output, which is that of goods only). The resulting productivity in the agricultural and non-agricultural sector is shown in Table 18 (the third column is obtained by dividing the first column by the second).

TABLE 18
Changes in productivity in agriculture and non-agriculture
from 1960 to 1965

	National output of goods	*Employment in full labour weeks Index 1965 (1960 = 100)*	*Productivity Index 1965 (1960 = 100)*
Agriculture	175	118	148
Non-agriculture (exclusive of services)	190	162	117

It will be seen that the increase in productivity in the non-agricultural sector is very low (approximately 3 per cent *per annum*), especially as contrasted with agriculture. A problem arises as to whether the assumption of stability of the labour force in agriculture was justified and whether some increase in it would not be warranted. It should be stated, however, that rural underemployment in 1960 does not find its full expression in statistics of employment and therefore the increase in employment in terms of full labour weeks is underestimated and the increase in productivity per full labour week is exaggerated.

The low rate of increase in productivity in the non-agricultural sector arrived at above seems to point to the following conclusions.

(*a*) No emphasis should be laid on application of labour saving techniques in the next five year period.

(*b*) Even so the actual increase in productivity may well be higher than that reached above on the basis of the rate of growth postulated in this plan and the assumption of achieving full employment by 1965. If such a situation were to arise it would be advisable to reduce the working time so as to sustain full employment without artificially curbing the natural increase in productivity.

(*c*) Should such a course be taken, the reduction of working hours must be organised in such a way as not to reduce the degree of utilisation of capital equipment.

NOTES AND REFERENCES

1. Except for burning of *bagasse*, the admixture of alcohol to gasoline, and some hydroelectricity; the utilisation of the deposits of pit has not been sufficiently explored to be taken into consideration.
2. If the production of fishmeal in 1965 were included, the increase would be five times. However, fishmeal being used for fodder should not be included in the joint final product of agriculture and fishing.
3. See his book *Programa nacional de producción de grasas comestibles 1960–70*. The results arrived at there were used by him in preparing the five year plan for agriculture.

II

Bolivia—An
'Intermediate Regime'
in Latin America*

❃

I

One of the co-authors of this paper, M. Kalecki, has used the term 'intermediate regimes' to characterise a number of under-developed countries which achieved independence after the Second World War, encroached to a considerable extent upon foreign interests, carried out an agrarian reform, embarked on a process of economic development with significant participation of the government—and which cannot be considered either strictly capitalist or socialist.[1]

He thought that the governments in these countries repre-sented the interests of lower-middle class and rich or medium-rich peasants amalgamated with state capitalism (the managers of the government sector also come mostly from the middle classes). The antagonists of these governments from above are the remnants of feudalism left over after the agrarian reform and the native big business (often reduced in scope by nationa-lisation). The antagonists from below are poor peasants and agricultural workers, who in general profit little from the land reform, and the urban paupers: people without stable employ-ment, home workers and workers in small establishments. White collar workers and workers in large establishments—who are in a rather privileged position as compared with rural and urban paupers—frequently support the intermediate regimes, especially when employed in state enterprises.

* Written in collaboration with Marcin Kula. First published in *Econo-mia y Administración*, 1970 (16), 75–8.

The foreign policy of non-alignment of the intermediate regimes was in a sense a counterpart to their internal set-up. At the same time neutrality between two blocs is very important from the point of view of reinforcing the bargaining position in negotiations for foreign credits or technical assistance.

II

The countries referred to above are situated in the Far East, Middle East and Africa, with India and Egypt as the most characteristic examples. In Latin America, all countries have had independence for a long time, at least formally, and the Second World War did not basically change conditions there. The advent of the intermediate regime in 1952 in Bolivia was different in character from that in the above countries. The 'revolution' under the leadership of Paz Estenssoro came about as a result of the alliance of certain forces opposing the oligarchy based on the tin mining concerns and the feudal landlords. This alliance consisted of some radical nationalists among the intelligentsia, army officers and the tin miners, a very poor and exploited class (recruited from rural paupers). It should be noticed that the countryside was dominated by typical feudalism (which did not produce for export) and that large-scale manufacturing was non-existent.

The beginning of the revolution was characterised by two measures typical of the intermediate regimes: nationalisation of the tin mines, which were owned by a combination of foreign and native capital, and an agrarian reform. It is true that the latter was by no means perfect, especially in its execution. But on this point Bolivia did not differ much from other intermediate regimes. And it had two consequences which it shares with the countries referred to above:

(*a*) It created a rather vigorous stratum of rich or medium-rich peasants;

(*b*) It broke the feudal landlords as a ruling class, transforming them into a rather ineffectual right-wing opposition to the regime. The government subsequently embarked on a scheme of economic development.

III

As will be seen, the participation of the Bolivian tin miners (and their trade unions) in a sense replaced the fight for independence as a motive force in the upheaval of 1952. As a result, the miners were represented in the government by their leader and their wages were increased. In consequence of the subsequent inflation—which occurred for various reasons not analysed here—and the method of 'curing' it by a US inspired 'stabilisation programme', the real wages of the miners fell again to the previous extremely low level. (The justification of this by the high costs of production of the Bolivian tin ore is fallacious because a subsidy financed out of the general budget could have been applied; however, the stabilisation programme was generally *laissez faire* in character.) This led to a strike movement which was ruthlessly suppressed. The final outcome was the take-over by a military junta under General Barrientos in 1964, which continued the repression against miners.

At this point, an impression may arise that the intermediate regime went astray. The opposite, however, seems to be the case. It was the strong participation of the miners in the first phase of the 'revolutionary government' that constituted an anomaly for an intermediate regime. What subsequently happened to these miners is analogous to the rough deal that communists in general get in intermediate regimes, because they are at least potential spokesmen for the rural and urban paupers.[2] Viewed in this way, the counterrevolutionary shift to the right was in fact a 'normalisation' of an intermediate regime. It is true, however, that this shift was precipitated by US influence.

IV

As contrasted with other intermediate regimes, Bolivia did not practise non-alignment (if we abstract from some attempts in the early stage of revolution). Indeed it could be satisfied that the USA did not interfere drastically with its revolution—a striking contrast with the treatment of Guatemala under Arbenz. What was the reason for this tolerant attitude? First, it was important that no concern with a powerful lobby in the USA, like the United Fruit Co., was engaged in Bolivia. The tin mining interests had no such powerful connexions; and the agrarian reform did not interfere with any US plantations because such were non-existent. Capturing the nationalised tin mines was not a very attractive proposition because, being to a considerable extent exhausted, they are definitely high cost producers. In addition, the ores are customarily sold on the American market and no smelting facilities are available on the spot. Where, however, promising raw material resources, for instance oil, were available, a concession to US concerns was granted at a later stage. (However, Bolivian internal demand was covered by a government operated concern.)

Secondly, throughout the period considered Bolivia was dependent on the 'economic assistance' of the USA, which thus could exert a powerful influence upon its internal development (see section III).

Nevertheless, tin mining has not been denationalised or the agrarian reform reversed. After the new *coup d'état* by General Ovando Candia (an earlier associate of Barrientos) in 1969 even the oil concessions were partly cancelled. *Per saldo* the intermediate regime (which should by no means be confused with socialism) has been maintained, despite the fact that Bolivia has remained in the US sphere of influence.

V

One of the inferences from the above is an explanation of the fate of Che Guevara guerilla movement in Bolivia. It is clear that when choosing the field of his activities in Latin America he did not make an adequate analysis of the social and economic realities of the 'battleground'. A guerilla movement succeeds, first and foremost, in a region where poor peasants and agricultural workers are oppressed by feudal landlords. A classical guerilla movement tends to develop into a peasant war. But in Bolivia the situation was nearly the reverse of this, as is symbolised by the distribution of arms by General Barrientos to peasants of the region of Cochabamba for use against the guerillas.

It is true that there was a theoretical possibility of support for the guerillas from miners whose fight against the government reached a peak at the time of Che Guevara's activity (but independently of it). In actual fact, however, they could not *feed* the guerillas. Although the miners were recruited from poor peasants, they *are* not poor peasants. They do not produce food. On the contrary, even strike actions are difficult because of the possibility of blocking the supply of food to the miners. Only an alliance of miners and peasants could be a basis for rebellion, but that was hardly possible; in 1952 the miners, allied with radical elements of intelligentsia and the officer corps, brought about the overthrow of the traditional oligarchy. The ensuing agrarian reform worked against the alliance of miners and peasants in the next phase, inadequate though it was. In the circumstances, Che Guevara's undertaking was doomed.

VI

Is Bolivia an isolated instance of an intermediate regime in Latin America or a pattern that will spread to other countries of that subcontinent? There is a temptation to discover the outlines of this pattern in a recent revolution in Peru, but some doubts arise at least in the present stage. It is true the revolutionary officers' junta declared nationalisation of the oilfields and also a far-reaching agrarian reform. The latter, however, is being carried out for the time being only in the littoral North, where plantations of sugar cane are situated, which were nationalised. (This may be to some extent directed against the Apra party, which is the organiser of the trade unions of the plantation workers.) As to the land in the mountains, which is the proper domain of the feudal landlords, progress is for the time being small. Apart from this there exists in Peru, as contrasted with Bolivia, big industrial business with strong US connexions. The most prominent example is the production of fish meal, which is one of the main export items.

It is probable that in many Latin American countries the industrial big business, associated with feudal elements, is already too strong to leave the door open for an intermediate regime; and that in these countries capitalism will develop according to the 'Prussian pattern', maintaining close relations with US concerns. Indeed, one of the conditions of the appearance of intermediate regimes in the Far East, Middle East and Africa was the weakness of native industrial big business[3] in relation to the very numerous lower-middle class.

NOTES AND REFERENCES

1. In a paper published first in Polish in 1964; an expanded version covering the events in Indonesia appeared in Polish in 1966 and in English in *Co-existence*, No. 1, 1967 [reproduced as Chapter 4 above].
2. *Cf.* pp. 34–5 above.
3. In Bolivia the industrial big business (exclusive of traditional tin mining) was, as said above, non-existent.

Index

Index

Index

Mexico, 123
Millikan, Max F., 92
Mixed economy, and perspective planning, 28–9; foreign trade in, 107–11
Moneylenders, *see* Capitalists
Monopoly, 50
Montevideo Treaty, 88, 97

El-Naggar, Said, 93
Nasser, Gamal Abdul-, 34
National income, and foreign credits, 111–15; growth of, 99–101, 104, 107–8, 147–8, 150; and investment, 21, 101–3
Nationalisation, 198, 199, 202
NATO, 92
Necessities, 98; demand and supply of, 17–18, 24–6, 68–9, 99–100, 104–5, 111, 147, 148; expenditure on, 152–3; and foreign credits, 113–15; imports of, 70, 107–8; price increases of, 105–7; production of, 107–8, 111–13
Nehru, Jawaharlal, 34
Neo-classical economic theory, 7
New York Times, 92
Non-essentials, 52, 65, 68–9; production of, 70, 73; taxation of, 98, 100, 103–5, 111, 113–14, 143, 148, 151–3

Oil, 19, 83, 130
Oil-producing countries, 107, 108
Oil refining, 168, 171–2

Patents, 84
Paupers, 33, 34–5, 198, 200
Peasantry, and capitalists, 19, 26, 28, 33, 34, 104; poor, 33, 34–5, 36; rich, 30, 32, 34, 37, 198
Peru, 202
'Pick and shovel' employment, 17–18
Planned economy, 25–7, 32
Planning Commission, Perspective Planning Division (Cuba), 152
Prebisch, Raul, 91, 96
Price stabilisation, 87–8
Private foreign investment, 80–5, 93

Prochorov, G. M., 93
Productive capacity, 44–5; expansion of, 23–5, 70; and foreign aid, 65–6, 90; reserves of, 46, 124, 125, 169–70
Productivity, 18, 195–6; increase in, 48–51
Profits, of foreign investment, 81–2, 84; savings of, 21; taxation of, 9, 22, 24, 60
'Propensity to consume', 8

Quintana, Carlos, 170

Raj, K. N., 10–11, 93, 94
Ranis, G., 91
Raw materials, 88, 125, 127, 129; imports of, 52, 55; production of, 56, 131–2; substitution of, 132
Religion, 35
Resources, underutilisation of, 20–2
Rosenstein-Rodan, P., 90, 91
Rural migration, 47, 49–50

Sachs, Ignacy, 11, 64
Santamaria, Carlos Sanz de, 91, 96
Savings, 21, 41–2, 144; 'forced', 44; and investment, 43–5, 151, 153–4; and taxation, 59
Service cooperatives, 19
Socialist economies, credits from, 32, 75, 88; perspective planning in, 28–9
Soviet Union, 75, 94
Staple foods, 98, 104
State capitalism, 31–2
State interventionism, 30–1
Subsidies, 131, 140, 141
Surplus, realisation of, 8
Surplus imports, 11–12

Taxation, 10, 18, 25, 26, 29, 143; as anti-inflationary measure, 58–60; and foreign aid, 69–70; of foreign investment, 84; and full employment, 22; of higher income groups, 98, 100, 103–5, 111, 113–14, 147; and investment, 52–4, 100, 103–5, 151–2; of